Pass the Accuplacer!

Accuplacer® Exam Study Guide and Practice Test Questions

Published by

Complete TEST Preparation Inc.

Version 6.5 April 2015

Version 6.5 April 2015

Pass the Accuplacer!

Accuplacer® Exam Study Guide and Practice Test Questions

Published by

Complete TEST Preparation Inc.

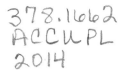
We strongly recommend that students check with exam providers for up-to-date information regarding test content.

ISBN: 9781928077770

Published by
Complete Test Preparation Inc.
921 Foul Bay Rd.
Victoria BC Canada V8S 4H9
Visit us on the web at http://www.test-preparation.ca
Printed in the USA

About Complete Test Preparation Inc.

Complete Test Preparation Inc. has been publishing high quality study materials since 2005. Thousands of students visit our websites every year, and thousands of students, teachers and parents all over the world have purchased our teaching materials, curriculum, study guides and practice tests.

Complete Test Preparation Inc. is committed to providing students with the best study materials and practice tests available on the market. Members of our team combine years of teaching experience, with experienced writers and editors, all with advanced degrees.

Team Members for this publication

Editor: Brian Stocker MA
Contributor: Dr. C. Gregory
Contributor: Dr. G. A. Stocker DDS
Contributor: D. A. Stocker M. Ed.
Contributor: Elizabeta Petrovic MSc (Mathematics)
Contributor: Kelley O'Malley BA (English)

The Environment and Sustainability

Environmental consciousness is important for the continued growth of our company. Besides eco-balancing each title, as a print on demand publisher, we only print units as orders come in, which greatly reduces excess printing and waste. This revolutionary printing technology also eliminates carbon emissions from trucks hauling boxes of books everywhere to warehouses. We also maintain a commitment to recycling any waste materials that may result from the printing process. We continue to review our manufacturing practices on an ongoing basis to ensure we are doing our part to protect and improve the environment.

Feedback

We welcome your feedback. Email us at feedback@test-preparation.ca with your comments and suggestions. We carefully review all suggestions and often incorporate reader suggestions into upcoming versions. As a Print on Demand Publisher, we update our products frequently.

 Find us on Facebook
www.facebook.com/CompleteTestPreparation

Contents

Getting Started

CONGRATULATIONS! By deciding to take the Accuplacer® Exam, you have taken the first step toward a great future! Of course, there is no point in taking this important examination unless you intend to do your very best to earn the highest grade you possibly can. That means getting yourself organized and discovering the best approaches, methods and strategies to master the material. Yes, that will require real effort and dedication on your part, but if you are willing to focus your energy and devote the study time necessary, before you know it you will be on you will be opening that letter of acceptance to the school of your dreams!

We know that taking on a new endeavour can be a little scary, and it is easy to feel unsure of where to begin. That's where we come in. This study guide is designed to help you improve your test-taking skills, show you a few tricks of the trade and increase both your competency and confidence.

The Accuplacer® Exam

The Accuplacer® exam is composed of four sections, reading, mathematics, sentence skills and writing. The reading section consists of reading comprehension questions. The mathematics section contains three sections, arithmetic, algebra and college level math. The sentence skills section contains questions on sentence structure and rewriting sentences. The writing section contains an essay question.

While we seek to make our guide as comprehensive as possible, note that like all exams, the Accuplacer® Exam might be adjusted at some future point. New material might be added, or content that is no longer relevant or applicable might be removed. It is always a good idea to give the materials you receive when you register to take the Accuplacer® a careful review.

How this study guide is organized

This study guide is divided into four sections. The first section, Self-Assessments, which will help you recognize your areas of strength and weaknesses. This will be a boon when it comes to managing your study time most efficiently; there is not much point of focusing on material you have already got firmly under control. Instead, taking the self-assessments will show you where that time could be much better spent. In this area you will begin with a few questions to evaluate quickly your understanding of material that is likely to appear on the Accuplacer®. If you do poorly in certain areas, simply work carefully through those sections in the tutorials and then try the self-assessment again.

The second section, Tutorials, offers information in each of the content areas, as well as strategies to help you master that material. The tutorials are not intended to be a complete course, but cover general principles. If you find that you do not understand the tutorials, it is recommended that you seek out additional instruction.

Third, we offer two sets of practice test questions, similar to those on the Accuplacer® Exam.

The Accuplacer® Study Plan

Now that you have made the decision to take the Accuplacer®, it is time to get started. Before you do another thing, you will need to figure out a plan of attack. The very best study tip is to start early! The longer the time period you devote to regular study practice, the more likely you will retain the material and be able to access it quickly. If you thought that

1x20 is the same as 2x10, guess what? It really is not, when it comes to study time. Reviewing material for just an hour per day over the course of 20 days is far better than studying for two hours a day for only 10 days. The more often you revisit a particular piece of information, the better you will know it. Not only will your grasp and understanding be better, but your ability to reach into your brain and quickly and efficiently pull out the tidbit you need, will be greatly enhanced as well.

The great Chinese scholar and philosopher Confucius believed that true knowledge could be defined as knowing both what you know and what you do not know. The first step in preparing for the Accuplacer® is to assess your strengths and weaknesses. You may already have an idea of what you know and what you do not know, but evaluating yourself using our Self- Assessment modules for each of the three areas, Math, Writing and Reading Comprehension, will clarify the details.

Making a Study Schedule

To make your study time most productive, you will need to develop a study plan. The purpose of the plan is to organize all the bits of pieces of information in such a way that you will not feel overwhelmed. Rome was not built in a day, and learning everything you will need to know to pass the Accuplacer® is going to take time, too. Arranging the material you need to learn into manageable chunks is the best way to go. Each study session should make you feel as though you have succeeded in accomplishing your goal, and your goal is simply to learn what you planned to learn during that particular session. Try to organize the content in such a way that each study session builds on previous ones. That way, you will retain the information, be better able to access it, and review the previous bits and pieces at the same time.

Self-assessment

The Best Study Tip! The very best study tip is to start early! The longer you study regularly, the more you will retain and 'learn' the material. Studying for 1 hour per day for 20 days is far better than studying for 2 hours for 10 days.

What don't you know?

The first step is to assess your strengths and weaknesses. You may already have an idea of where your weaknesses are, or you can take our Self-assessment modules for each of the areas, Reading Comprehension, Arithmetic, Essay Writing, Algebra and College Level Math.

Exam Component	Rate 1 to 5
Reading Comprehension	
Making Inferences	
Main idea	
Arithmetic	
Decimals Percent and Fractions	
Problem solving (Word Problems)	
Basic Algebra	
Simple Geometry	
Problem Solving	
Essay Writing	
Sentence Skills	
Sentence Correction	
Sentence Shift	
Basic English Grammar and Usage	

Algebra	
Exponents	
Linear Equations	
Quadratics	
Polynomials	
College Level	
Coordinate Geometry	
Trigonometry	
Polynomials	
Logarithms	
Sequences	

Making a Study Schedule

The key to making a study plan is to divide the material you need to learn into manageable size and learn it, while at the same time reviewing the material that you already know.

Using the table above, any scores of three or below, you need to spend time learning, going over and practicing this subject area. A score of four means you need to review the material, but you don't have to spend time re-learning. A score of five and you are OK with just an occasional review before the exam.

A score of zero or one means you really do need to work on this and you should allocate the most time and give it the highest priority. Some students prefer a 5-day plan and others a 10-day plan. It also depends on how much time you have until the exam.

Here is an example of a 5-day plan based on an example from the table above:

Main Idea: 1 Study 1 hour everyday – review on last day
Fractions: 3 Study 1 hour for 2 days then ½ hour and then review

Algebra: 4   Review every second day
Grammar & Usage: 2 Study 1 hour on the first day – then ½ hour everyday
Reading Comprehension: 5   Review for ½ hour every other day
Geometry: 5 Review for ½ hour every other day

Using this example, geometry and reading comprehension are good and only need occasional review. Algebra is good and needs 'some' review. Fractions need a bit of work, grammar and usage needs a lot of work and Main Idea is very weak and need most of time. Based on this, here is a sample study plan:

Day	Subject	Time
Monday		
Study	Main Idea	1 hour
Study	Grammar & Usage	1 hour
	½ hour break	
Study	Fractions	1 hour
Review	Algebra	½ hour
Tuesday		
Study	Main Idea	1 hour
Study	Grammar & Usage	½ hour
	½ hour break	
Study	Fractions	½ hour
Review	Algebra	½ hour
Review	Geometry	½ hour
Wednesday		
Study	Main Idea	1 hour
Study	Grammar & Usage	½ hour
	½ hour break	
Study	Fractions	½ hour
Review	Geometry	½ hour
Thursday		
Study	Main Idea	½ hour
Study	Grammar & Usage	½ hour
Review	Fractions	½ hour
	½ hour break	

Review	Geometry	½ hour
Review	Algebra	½ hour
Friday		
Review	Main Idea	½ hour
Review	Grammar & Usage	½ hour
Review	Fractions	½ hour
	½ hour break	
Review	Algebra	½ hour
Review	Grammar & Usage	½ hour

Using this example, adapt the study plan to your own schedule. This schedule assumes 2 ½ - 3 hours available to study everyday for a 5 day period.

First, write out what you need to study and how much. Next figure out how many days you have before the test. Note, do NOT study on the last day before the test. On the last day before the test, you won't learn anything and will probably only confuse yourself.

Make a table with the days before the test and the number of hours you have available to study each day. We suggest working with 1 hour and ½ hour time slots.

Start filling in the blanks, with the subjects you need to study the most getting the most time and the most regular time slots (i.e. everyday) and the subjects that you know getting the least time (i.e. ½ hour every other day, or every 3rd day).

Tips for making a schedule

Once you make a schedule, stick with it! Make your study sessions reasonable. If you make a study schedule and don't stick with it, you set yourself up for failure. Instead, schedule study sessions that are a bit shorter and set yourself up for success! Make sure your study sessions are do-able. Studying is hard work but after you pass, you can party and take a break!

Schedule breaks. Breaks are just as important as study

time. Work out a rotation of studying and breaks that works for you.

Build up study time.   If you find it hard to sit still and study for 1 hour straight through, build up to it. Start with 20 minutes, and then take a break. Once you get used to 20-minute study sessions, increase the time to 30 minutes. Gradually work you way up to 1 hour.

40 minutes to 1 hour is optimal.   Studying for longer than this is tiring and not productive. Studying for shorter isn't long enough to be productive.

Studying Math.   Studying Math is different from studying other subjects because you use a different part of your brain. The best way to study math is to practice everyday. This will train your mind to think in a mathematical way. If you miss a day or days, the mathematical mind-set is gone, and you have to start all over again to build it up.

Study and practice math everyday for at least 5 days before the exam.

Reading Comprehension

THIS SECTION CONTAINS A SELF-ASSESSMENT AND READING TUTORIAL. The tutorials are designed to familiarize general principles and the self-assessment contains general questions similar to the reading questions likely to be on the Accuplacer®, but are not intended to be identical to the exam questions. The tutorials are not designed to be a complete reading course, and it is assumed that students have some familiarity with reading comprehension questions. If you do not understand parts of the tutorial, or find the tutorial difficult, it is recommended that you seek out additional instruction.

Tour of the Accuplacer® Reading Comprehension Content

The Accuplacer® reading section has 25 reading comprehension questions. Below is a detailed list of the types of reading comprehension questions that generally appear on the Accuplacer®.

- Draw logical conclusions

- Identify the main idea

- Identify secondary ideas

- Identify the author's intent

In the second section, you are given 2 sentences and are asked to identify the relationship between the sentences. The relationship may consist of a:

- Comparison

- Contrast

- Contradiction

- Solution

- Example

- Repetition

- Effect

- Analysis

- Re-statement

- Conclusion

The questions below are not the same as you will find on the Accuplacer® - that would be too easy! And nobody knows what the questions will be and they change all the time. Mostly the changes consist of substituting new questions for old, but the changes can be new question formats or styles, changes to the number of questions in each section, changes to the time limits for each section and combining sections. Below are general reading questions that cover the same areas as the Accuplacer®. So, while the format and exact wording of the questions may differ slightly, and change from year to year, if you can answer the questions below, you will have no problem with the reading section of the Accuplacer®.

Reading Comprehension Self-Assessment

The purpose of the self-assessment is:

- Identify your strengths and weaknesses.

- Develop your personalized study plan (above)

- Get accustomed to the Accuplacer® format

- Extra practice – the self-assessments are almost a full 3rd practice test!

- Provide a baseline score for preparing your study schedule.

Since this is a Self-assessment, and depending on how confident you are with Reading Comprehension, timing is optional. The Accuplacer® has 25 reading questions. The self-assessment has 24 questions, so allow about 20 minutes to complete this assessment.

Once complete, use the table below to assess your understanding of the content, and prepare your study schedule described in chapter 1.

80% - 100%	Excellent – you have mastered the content
60 – 79%	Good. You have a working knowledge. Even though you can just pass this section, you may want to review the tutorials and do some extra practice to see if you can improve your mark.
40% - 59%	Below Average. You do not understand reading comprehension problems. Review the tutorials , and retake this quiz again in a few days, before proceeding to the practice test questions.

Less than 40%	Poor. You have a very limited under-standing of reading comprehension problems. Please review the tutorials , and retake this quiz again in a few days, before proceeding to the practice test questions.

Reading Self-Assessment Answer Sheet

1. Ⓐ Ⓑ Ⓒ Ⓓ   11. Ⓐ Ⓑ Ⓒ Ⓓ   21. Ⓐ Ⓑ Ⓒ Ⓓ

2. Ⓐ Ⓑ Ⓒ Ⓓ   12. Ⓐ Ⓑ Ⓒ Ⓓ   22. Ⓐ Ⓑ Ⓒ Ⓓ

3. Ⓐ Ⓑ Ⓒ Ⓓ   13. Ⓐ Ⓑ Ⓒ Ⓓ   23. Ⓐ Ⓑ Ⓒ Ⓓ

4. Ⓐ Ⓑ Ⓒ Ⓓ   14. Ⓐ Ⓑ Ⓒ Ⓓ   24. Ⓐ Ⓑ Ⓒ Ⓓ

5. Ⓐ Ⓑ Ⓒ Ⓓ   15. Ⓐ Ⓑ Ⓒ Ⓓ

6. Ⓐ Ⓑ Ⓒ Ⓓ   16. Ⓐ Ⓑ Ⓒ Ⓓ

7. Ⓐ Ⓑ Ⓒ Ⓓ   17. Ⓐ Ⓑ Ⓒ Ⓓ

8. Ⓐ Ⓑ Ⓒ Ⓓ   18. Ⓐ Ⓑ Ⓒ Ⓓ

9. Ⓐ Ⓑ Ⓒ Ⓓ   19. Ⓐ Ⓑ Ⓒ Ⓓ

10. Ⓐ Ⓑ Ⓒ Ⓓ   20. Ⓐ Ⓑ Ⓒ Ⓓ

Questions 1 – 4 refer to the following passage.

Passage 1 - Who Was Anne Frank?

You may have heard mention of the word Holocaust in your History or English classes. The Holocaust took place from 1939-1945. It was an attempt by the Nazi party to purify the human race, by eliminating Jews, Gypsies, Catholics, homosexuals and others they deemed inferior to their "perfect" Aryan race. The Nazis used Concentration Camps, which were sometimes used as Death Camps, to exterminate the people they held in the camps. The saddest fact about the Holocaust was the over one million children under the age of sixteen died in a Nazi concentration camp. Just a few weeks before World War II was over, Anne Frank was one of those children to die.

Before the Nazi party began its persecution of the Jews, Anne Frank had a happy live. She was born in June of 1929. In June of 1942, for her 13th birthday, she was given a simple present which would go onto impact the lives of millions of people around the world. That gift was a small red diary that she called Kitty. This diary was to become Anne's most treasured possession when she and her family hid from the Nazi's in a secret annex above her father's office building in Amsterdam.

For 25 months, Anne, her sister Margot, her parents, another family, and an elderly Jewish dentist hid from the Nazis in this tiny annex. They were never permitted to go outside and their food and supplies were brought to them by Miep Gies and her husband, who did not believe in the Nazi persecution of the Jews. It was a very difficult life for young Anne and she used Kitty as an outlet to describe her life in hiding. After 2 years, Anne and her family were betrayed and arrested by the Nazis. To this day, nobody is exactly sure who betrayed the Frank family and the other annex residents. Anne, her mother, and her sister were separated from Otto Frank, Anne's father. Then, Anne and Margot were separated from their mother. In March of 1945, Margot Frank died of starvation in a Concentration Camp. A few days later, at the age of 15, Anne Frank died of typhus. Of all the people who hid in the Annex, only Otto Frank survived the Holocaust.

Otto Frank returned to the Annex after World War II. It was there that he found Kitty, filled with Anne's thoughts and feelings about being a persecuted Jewish girl. Otto Frank had Anne's diary published in 1947 and it has remained continuously in print ever since. Today, the diary has been published in over 55 languages and more than 24 million copies have been sold around the world. The Diary of Anne Frank tells the story of a brave young woman who tried to see the good in all people.

1. From the context clues in the passage, the word Annex most nearly means?

    a. Attic

    b. Bedroom

    c. Basement

    d. Kitchen

2. Why do you think Anne's diary has been published in 55 languages?

    a. So everyone could understand it.

    b. So people around the world could learn more about the horrors of the Holocaust.

    c. Because Anne was Jewish but hid in Amsterdam and died in Germany.

    d. Because Otto Frank spoke many languages.

3. From the description of Anne and Margot's deaths in the passage, what can we assume typhus is?

    a. The same as starving to death.

    b. An infection the Germans gave to Anne.

    c. A disease Anne caught in the concentration camp.

    d. Poison gas used by the Germans to kill Anne.

4. In the third paragraph, what does the word outlet most nearly mean?

a. A place to plug things into the wall

b. A store where Miep bought cheap supplies for the Frank family

c. A hiding space similar to an Annex

d. A place where Anne could express her private thoughts.

Questions 5 – 8 refer to the following passage.

Passage 2 - Was Dr. Seuss A Real Doctor?

A favorite author for over 100 years, Theodor Seuss Geisel was born on March 2, 1902. Today, we celebrate the birthday of the famous "Dr. Seuss" by hosting Read Across America events throughout the March. School children around the country celebrate the "Doctor's" birthday by making hats, giving presentations and holding read aloud circles featuring some of Dr. Seuss' most famous books.

But who was Dr. Seuss? Did he go to medical school? Where was his office? You may be surprised to know that Theodor Seuss Geisel was not a medical doctor at all. He took on the nickname Dr. Seuss when he became a noted children's book author. He earned the nickname because people said his books were "as good as medicine." All these years later, his nickname has lasted and he is known as Dr. Seuss all across the world.

Think back to when you were a young child. Did you ever want to try "green eggs and ham?" Did you try to "Hop on Pop?" Do you remember learning about the environment from a creature called The Lorax? Of course, you must recall one of Seuss' most famous characters; that green Grinch who stole Christmas. These stories were all written by Dr. Seuss and featured his signature rhyming words and letters. They also featured made up words to enhance his rhyme scheme and even though many of his characters were made up, they sure seem real to us today.

And what of his "signature" book, The Cat in the Hat? You must remember that cat and Thing One and Thing Two from your childhood. Did you know that in the early 1950's there was a growing concern in America that children were not becoming avid readers? This was, book publishers thought, because children found books dull and uninteresting. An intelligent publisher sent Dr. Seuss a book of words that he thought all children should learn as young readers. Dr. Seuss wrote his famous story The Cat in the Hat, using those words. We can see, over the decades, just how much influence his writing has had on very young children. That is why we celebrate this doctor's birthday each March.

5. What does the word "avid" mean in the last paragraph?

    a. Good

    b. Interested

    c. Slow

    d. Fast

6. What can we infer from the statement " His books were like medicine?"

    a. His books made people feel better

    b. His books were in doctor's office waiting rooms

    c. His books took away fevers

    d. His books left a funny taste in readers' mouths.

7. Why is the publisher in the last paragraph referred to as "intelligent?"

    a. The publisher knew how to read.

    b. The publisher knew kids did not like to read.

    c. The publisher knew Dr. Seuss would be able to create a book that sold well.

    d. The publisher knew that Dr. Seuss would be able to write a book that would get young children interested in reading.

8. The theme of this passage is

a. Dr. Seuss was not a doctor.

b. Dr. Seuss influenced the lives of generations of young children.

c. Dr. Seuss wrote rhyming books.

d. Dr. Suess' birthday is a good day to read a book.

Questions 9 – 12 refer to the following passage.

Keeping Tropical Fish

Keeping tropical fish at home or in your office used to be very popular. Today, interest has declined, but it remains as rewarding and relaxing a hobby as ever. Ask any tropical fish hobbyist, and you will hear how soothing and relaxing watching colorful fish live their lives in the aquarium. If you are considering keeping tropical fish as pets, here is a list of the basic equipment you will need.

A filter is essential for keeping your aquarium clean and your fish alive and healthy. There are different types and sizes of filters and the right size for you depends on the size of the aquarium and the level of stocking. Generally, you need a filter with a 3 to 5 times turn over rate per hour. This means that the water in the tank should go through the filter about 3 to 5 times per hour.

Most tropical fish do well in water temperatures ranging between 24^0 C and 26^0 C, though each has its own ideal water temperature. A heater with a thermostat is necessary to regulate the water temperature. Some heaters are submersible and others are not, so check carefully before you buy.

Lights are also necessary, and come in a large variety of types, strengths and sizes. A light source is necessary for plants in the tank to photosynthesize and give the tank a more attractive appearance. Even if you plan to use plastic plants, the fish still require light, although here you can use a lower strength light source.

A hood is necessary to keep dust, dirt and unwanted materials out of the tank. Sometimes the hood can also help prevent evaporation. Another requirement is aquarium gravel. This will improve the aesthetics of the aquarium and is necessary if you plan to have real plants.

9. What is the general tone of this article?

    a. Formal

    b. Informal

    c. Technical

    d. Opinion

10. Which of the following cannot be inferred?

    a. Gravel is good for aquarium plants.

    b. Fewer people have aquariums in their office than at home.

    c. The larger the tank, the larger the filter required.

    d. None of the above.

11. What evidence does the author provide to support their claim that aquarium lights are necessary?

    a. Plants require light.

    b. Fish and plants require light.

    c. The author does not provide evidence for this statement.

    d. Aquarium lights make the aquarium more attractive.

12. Which of the following is an opinion?

a. Filter with a 3 to 5 times turn over rate per hour are required.

b. Aquarium gravel improves the aesthetics of the aquarium.

c. An aquarium hood keeps dust, dirt and unwanted materials out of the tank.

d. Each type of tropical fish has its own ideal water temperature.

Questions 13 – 14 refer to the following passage.

Vice President Johnson, Mr. Speaker, Mr. Chief Justice, President Eisenhower, Vice President Nixon, President Truman, reverend clergy, fellow citizens:

We observe today not a victory of party, but a celebration of freedom -- symbolizing an end, as well as a beginning -- signifying renewal, as well as change. For I have sworn before you and Almighty God the same solemn oath our forebears prescribed nearly a century and three-quarters ago.

The world is very different now. For man holds in his mortal hands the power to abolish all forms of human poverty and all forms of human life. And yet the same revolutionary beliefs for which our forebears fought are still at issue around the globe -- the belief that the rights of man come not from the generosity of the state, but from the hand of God.

We dare not forget today that we are the heirs of that first revolution. Let the word go forth from this time and place, to friend and foe alike, that the torch has been passed to a new generation of Americans -- born in this century, tempered by war, disciplined by a hard and bitter peace, proud of our ancient heritage, and unwilling to witness or permit the slow undoing of those human rights to which this nation has always been committed, and to which we are committed today at home and around the world.

Let every nation know, whether it wishes us well or ill, that we shall pay any price, bear any burden, meet any hardship, support any friend, oppose any foe, to assure the survival and the success of liberty.

This much we pledge -- and more.

John F. Kennedy Inaugural Address 20 January 1961

13. What is the tone of this speech?

    a. Triumphant

    b. Optimistic

    c. Threatening

    d. Gloating

14. Which of the following is an opinion?

a. The world is very different now.

b. For man holds in his mortal hands the power to abolish all forms of human poverty and all forms of human life.

c. We dare not forget today that we are the heirs of that first revolution

d. For I have sworn before you and Almighty God the same solemn oath our forebears prescribed nearly a century and three-quarters ago.

15. Walt did not study for his English exam.

Walt failed his English exam, and his parents did not allow him to play his video games for a week.

a. The second sentence contrasts the first.

b. The second sentence restates an idea in the first sentence.

c. The second sentence states an effect.

d. The second sentence gives an example.

16. The flag of the United States and the flag of France are both red, white and blue.

The flag of the United States consists of stars and stripes but the flag of France does not.

    a. The second sentence restates an idea in the first sentence.

    b. The second sentence contrasts the first.

    c. The second sentence states an effect.

    d. The second sentence gives an example.

17. The jury deliberated for two hours.

A guilty verdict was reached.

    a. The second sentence reinforces the first.

    b. The second sentence analyzes a statement made in the first.

    c. The second sentence proposes a solution.

    d. The second sentence draws a conclusion.

18. Many fruits are commonly mistaken for vegetables.

Avocados, cucumbers, eggplant, okra, olives, peppers, pumpkin, squash and tomatoes are fruits that are mistaken for vegetables.

    a. The second sentence gives an example.

    b. The second sentence contrasts the first.

    c. The second sentence restates an idea in the first sentence.

    d. The second sentence states an effect.

19. Eating whole grains at least 3 three times a day reduces the risk of obesity, diabetes, heart disease, stroke and cancer.

Eating whole grains at least 3 three times a day reduces the risk of many chronic diseases.

    a. The second sentence contrasts the first.

    b. The second sentence restates an idea in the first sentence.

    c. The second sentence states an effect.

    d. The second sentence gives an example.

20. Robbie recited "Two roads diverged in a yellow wood, And sorry I could not travel both" to the class.

Ms. Frost said it means we must choose which path to take in life.

    a. The second sentence reinforces the first.

    b. The second sentence proposes a solution.

    c. The second sentence analyzes a statement made in the first.

    d. The second sentence draws a conclusion.

21. Queen Elizabeth II ended a centuries old British rule that puts boys before girls in the succession to the throne.

Queen Elizabeth II ended the centuries old royal succession law that made succession to the throne depended on gender, so now if Prince William and Kate Middleton, Duchess of Cambridge, have a girl first, she will become queen, and if she has any younger brothers, they will not be able to jump the line in succession of the throne.

    a. They express roughly the same idea.

    b. They contradict each other.

    c. They present problems and solutions.

    d. They establish a contrast.

22. California and Florida are both popular tourist destinations.

California's climate varies, but Florida's climate is mostly hot and humid.

    a. They express roughly the same idea.

    b. They establish a contrast.

    c. They contradict each other.

    d. They present problems and solutions.

23. Mary Boca said she is a strict vegetarian.

Mary said she ate a turkey wrap instead of a veggie wrap at the business luncheon.

    a. They express roughly the same idea.

    b. They establish a contrast.

    c. They contradict each other.

    d. They present problems and solutions.

24. Tennessee is well known for country music.

Many people think of Nashville when they think of country music, and Tennessee is the birthplace to many country music legends.

    a. They repeat the same idea.

    b. They contradict each other.

    c. They reinforce each other.

    d. They provide a problem and solution.

Reading Self-Assessment Answer Key

1. A
We know that an annex is like an attic because the text states the annex was above Otto Frank's building.

Option B is incorrect because an office building doesn't have bedrooms. Option C is incorrect because a basement would be below the office building. Option D is incorrect because there would not be a kitchen in an office building.

2. B
The diary has been published in 55 languages so people all over the world can learn about Anne. That is why the passage says it has been continuously in print.

Option A is incorrect because it is too vague. Option C is incorrect because it was published after Anne died and she did not write in all three languages. Option D is incorrect because the passage does not give us any information about what languages Otto Frank spoke.

3. C
Use the process of elimination to figure this out.

Option A cannot be the correct answer because otherwise the passage would have simply said that Anne and Margot both died of starvation. Options B and D cannot be correct because if the Germans had done something specifically to murder Anne, the passage would have stated that directly. By the process of elimination, Option C has to be the correct answer.

4. D
We can figure this out using context clues. The paragraph is talking about Anne's diary and so, outlet in this instance is a place where Anne can pour her feelings.

Option A is incorrect answer. That is the literal meaning of the word outlet and the passage is using the figurative meaning. Option B is incorrect because that is the secondary literal meaning of the word outlet, as in an outlet mall. Again, we are looking for figurative meaning. Option C is incorrect because there are no clues in the text to support that answer.

5. B
When someone is avid about something that means they are highly interested in the subject. The context clues are dull and boring, because they define the opposite of avid.

6. A
The author is using a simile to compare the books to medicine. Medicine is what you take when you want to feel better. They are suggesting that if a person wants to feel good, they should read Dr. Seuss' books.

Option B is incorrect because there is no mention of a doctor's office. Option C is incorrect because it is using the literal meaning of medicine and the author is using medicine in a figurative way. Option D is incorrect because it makes no sense. We know not to eat books.

7. D
The publisher is described as intelligent because he knew to get in touch with a famous author to develop a book that children would be interested in reading.

Option A is incorrect because we can assume that all book publishers must know how to read. Option B is incorrect because it says in the article that more than one publisher was concerned about whether or not children liked to read. Option D is incorrect because there is no mention in the article about how well The Cat in the Hat sold when it was first published.

8. B
The passage describes in detail how Dr. Seuss had a great effect on the lives of children through his writing. It names several of his books, tells how he helped children become avid readers and explains his style of writing.

Option A is incorrect because that is just one single fact about the passage. Option C is incorrect because that is just one single fact about the passage. Option D is incorrect because that is just one single fact about the passage. Again, Option B is correct because it encompasses ALL the facts in the passage, not just one single fact.

9. B
The general tone is informal.

10. B
The statement, "Fewer people have aquariums in their office than at home," cannot be inferred from this article.

11. C
The author does not provide evidence for this statement.

12. B
The following statement is an opinion, " Aquarium gravel improves the aesthetics of the aquarium."

13. A
This is a triumphant speech where President Kennedy is celebrating his victory.

14. C
The statement, "We dare not forget today that we are the heirs of that first revolution" is an opinion.

15. C
Walt did not study for his English exam.

Walt failed his English exam, and his parents did not allow him to play his video games for a week.

The second sentence states an effect.

Walt did not study for his English exam, so as a result he failed it, and his parents, as a form of punishment, did not allow him to play his video games for a week.

16. B
The flag of the United States and the flag of France are both red, white and blue.

The flag of the United States consists of stars and stripes but the flag of France does not.

The second sentence contrasts the first.

The second sentence describes the differences between the flags whereas the first compares similarities.

17. D
The jury deliberated for two hours.

A guilty verdict was reached.

The second sentence draws a conclusion.

The second sentence describes the outcome of the jury's deliberation.

18. A
Many fruits are commonly mistaken for vegetables.

Avocados, cucumbers, eggplant, okra, olives, peppers, pumpkin, squash and tomatoes are fruits that are mistaken for vegetables.

The second sentence gives an example.

The second sentence gives an example of fruits that are commonly mistaken for vegetables.

19. B
Eating whole grains at least 3 three times a day reduces the risk of obesity, diabetes, heart disease, stroke and cancer.

Eating whole grains at least 3 three times a day reduces the risk of many chronic diseases.

The second sentence restates an idea in the first sentence.

20. D
Robbie recited "Two roads diverged in a yellow wood, And sorry I could not travel both" to the class.

Ms. Frost said it means we must choose which path to take in life.

The second sentence analyzes a statement made in the first.

The second sentence analyzes a statement made in the first (a part of the first sentence).

21. A
Queen Elizabeth II ended a century of old British rule that puts boys before girls in the succession to the throne.

Queen Elizabeth II ended the centuries old royal succession law that made succession to the throne depended on gender, so now if Prince William and Kate Middleton, Duchess of Cambridge, have a girl first, she will become queen, and if she has any younger brothers, they will not be able to jump the line in succession of the throne.

They express roughly the same idea.

The ideas in both sentences are roughly the same.

22. B
California and Florida are both popular tourist destinations.

California's climate varies, but Florida's climate is mostly hot and humid.

They establish a contrast.

The second sentence describes the differences between California and Florida whereas the first compares their similarities.

23. C
Mary Boca said she is a strict vegetarian.

Mary said she ate a turkey wrap instead of a veggie wrap at the business luncheon.

The two sentences contradict each other.

24. C
Tennessee is well known for country music.

Many people think of Nashville when they think of country music, and Tennessee is the birthplace to many country music legends.

They reinforce each other.

The second sentence reinforces the first with supporting details.

Help with Reading Comprehension

At first sight, reading comprehension tests look challenging especially if you are given long essays to answer only two to three questions. While reading, you might notice your attention wandering, or you may feel sleepy. Do not be discouraged because there are various tactics and long range strategies that make comprehending even long, boring essays easier.

Your friends before your foes. It is always best to tackle essays or passages with familiar subjects rather than those with unfamiliar ones. This approach applies the same logic as tackling easy questions before hard ones. Skip passages that do not interest you and leave them for later when there is more time left.

Don't use 'special' reading techniques. This is not the time for speed-reading or anything like that – just plain ordinary reading – not too slow and not too fast.

Read through the entire passage and the questions before you do anything. Many students try reading the questions first and then looking for answers in the passage thinking this approach is more efficient. What these students do not realize is that it is often hard to navigate in unfamiliar roads. If you do not familiarize yourself with the passage first, looking for answers become not only time-consuming but also dangerous because you might miss the context of the answer you are looking for. If you read the questions first you will only confuse yourself and lose valuable time.

Familiarize yourself with reading comprehension questions. If you are familiar with the common types of reading questions, you are able to take note of important parts of the passage, saving time. There are six major kinds of reading questions.

> • **Main Idea**- Questions that ask for the central thought or significance of the passage.

- **Specific Details** - Questions that asks for explicitly stated ideas.

- **Drawing Inferences** - Questions that ask for a statement's intended meaning.

- **Tone or Attitude** - Questions that test your ability to sense the emotional state of the author.

- **Context Meaning** – Questions that ask for the meaning of a word depending on the context.

- **Technique** – Questions that ask for the method of organization or the writing style of the author.

Read. Read. Read. The best preparation for reading comprehension tests is always to read, read and read. If you are not used to reading lengthy passages, you will probably lose concentration. Increase your attention span by making a habit out of reading.

Reading Comprehension tests become less daunting when you have trained yourself to read and understand fast. Always remember that it is easier to understand passages you are interested in. Do not read through passages hastily. Make mental notes of ideas that you think might be asked.

Reading Strategy

When facing the reading comprehension section of a standardized test, you need a strategy to be successful. You want to keep several steps in mind:

- **First, make a note of the time and the number of sections**. Time your work accordingly. Typically, four to five minutes per section is sufficient. Second, read the directions for each selection thoroughly before beginning (and listen well to any additional verbal instructions, as they will often clarify obscure or confusing written guidelines). You must know exactly how to do what you're about to do!

• **Now you're ready to begin reading the selection**. Read the passage carefully, noting significant characters or events on a scratch sheet of paper or underlining on the test sheet. Many students find making a basic list in the margins helpful. Quickly jot down or underline one-word summaries of characters, notable happenings, numbers, or key ideas. This will help you better retain information and focus wandering thoughts. Remember, however, that your main goal in doing this is to find the information that answers the questions. Even if you find the passage interesting, remember your goal and work fast but stay on track.

• **Now read the question and all the options.** Now you have read the passage, have a general idea of the main ideas, and have marked the important points. Read the question and all the options. Never choose an answer without reading them all! Questions are often designed to confuse – stay focussed and clear. Usually the options will focus on one or two facts or inferences from the passage. Keep these clear in your mind.

• **Search for the answer**. With a very general idea of what the different options are, go back to the passage and scan for the relevant information. Watch for big words, unusual or unique words. These make your job easier as you can scan the text for the particular word.

• **Mark the Answer.** Now you have the key information the question is looking for. Go back to the question, quickly scan the options and mark the correct one.

Understand and practice the different types of standardized reading comprehension tests. See the list above for the different types. Typically, there will be several questions dealing with facts from the selection, a couple more inference questions dealing with logical consequences of those facts, and periodically an application-oriented question surfaces to force you to make connections with what you already know. Some students prefer to answer the questions as listed, and feel classifying the question and then ordering is wasting precious time. Other students prefer to answer the different types of questions in order of how easy or difficult they are. The choice is yours and do whatever works for you. If you want to try answering in order of difficulty, here is a recommended order, answer fact questions first; they're easily found within the passage. Tackle inference problems next, after re-reading the question(s) as many times as you need to. Application or 'best guess' questions usually take the longest, so save them for last.

Use the practice tests to try out both ways of answering and see what works for you.

For more help with reading comprehension, see Multiple Choice Secrets book at www.multiple choice.ca.

Main Idea and Supporting Details

Identifying the main idea, topic and supporting details in a passage can feel like an overwhelming task. The passages used for standardized tests can be boring and seem difficult - Test writers don't use interesting passages or ones that talk about things most people are familiar with. Despite these obstacles, all passages and paragraphs will have the information you need to answer the questions.

The topic of a passage or paragraph is its subject. It's the general idea and can be summed up in a word or short phrase. On some standardized tests, there is a short description of the passage if it's taken from a longer work. Make sure you read the description as it might state the topic of the passage. If not, read the passage and ask yourself, "Who or what is this about?" For example:

> Over the years, school uniforms have been
> hotly debated. Arguments are made that
> students have the right to show individuality

and express themselves by choosing their own clothes. However, this brings up social and academic issues. Some kids cannot afford to wear the clothes they like and might be bullied by the "better dressed" students. With attention drawn to clothes and the individual, students will lose focus on class work and the reason they are in school. School uniforms should be mandatory.

Ask: What is this paragraph about?

Topic: school uniforms

Once you have the topic, it's easier to find the main idea. The main idea is a specific statement telling what the writer wants you to know about the topic. Writers usually state the main idea as a thesis statement. If you're looking for the main idea of a single paragraph, the main idea is called the topic sentence and will probably be the first or last sentence. If you're looking for the main idea of an entire passage, look for the thesis statement in either the first or last paragraph. The main idea is usually restated in the conclusion. To find the main idea of a passage or paragraph, follow these steps:

1. Find the topic.

2. Ask yourself, "What point is the author trying to make about the topic?"

3. Create your own sentence summarizing the author's point.

4. Look in the text for the sentence closest in meaning to yours.

Look at the example paragraph again. It's already established that the topic of the paragraph is school uniforms. What is the main idea/topic sentence?

Ask: "What point is the author trying to make about school uniforms?"

Summary: Students should wear school uniforms.

Topic sentence: School uniforms should be mandatory.

Main Idea: School uniforms should be mandatory.

Each paragraph offers supporting details to explain the main idea. The details could be facts or reasons, but they will always answer a question about the main idea. What? Where? Why? When? How? How much/many? Look at the example paragraph again. You'll notice that more than one sentence answers a question about the main idea. These are the supporting details.

Main Idea: School uniforms should be mandatory.

Ask: Why? Some kids cannot afford to wear clothes they like and could be bullied by the "better dressed" kids. Supporting Detail

With attention drawn to clothes and the individual, Students will lose focus on class work and the reason they are in school. Supporting Detail

What if the author doesn't state the main idea in a topic sentence? The passage will have an implied main idea. It's not as difficult to find as it might seem. Paragraphs are always organized around ideas. To find an implied main idea, you need to know the topic and then find the relationship between the supporting details. Ask yourself, "What is the point the author is making about the relationship between the details?."

> Cocoa is what makes chocolate good for you. Chocolate comes in many varieties. These delectable flavors include milk chocolate, dark chocolate, semi-sweet, and white chocolate.

Ask: What is this paragraph about?

Topic: Chocolate

Ask: What? Where? Why? When? How? How much/many?

Supporting details: Chocolate is good for you because it is made of cocoa, Chocolate is delicious, Chocolate comes in different delicious flavors

Ask: What is the relationship between the details and what is the author's point?

Main Idea: Chocolate is good because it is healthy and it tastes good.

Testing Tips for Main Idea Questions

1. Skim the questions – not the answer options - before reading the passage.

2. Questions about main idea might use the words "theme," "generalization," or "purpose."

3. Save questions about the main idea for last. On standardized tests like the SAT, the answers to the rest of the questions can be found in order in the passage.

3. Underline topic sentences in the passage. Most tests allow you to write in your testing booklet.

4. Answer the question in your own words before looking at the options. Then match your answer with an option.

5. Cross out incorrect options immediately to prevent confusion.

6. If two of the options mean the same thing but use different words, they are BOTH incorrect.

7. If a question asks about the whole passage, cross out the options that apply only to part of it.

8. If only part of the information is correct, that option is incorrect.

9. An option that is too broad is incorrect. All information needs to be backed up by the passage.

10. Options with extreme wording are usually incorrect.

Arithmetic

THIS SECTION CONTAINS A SELF-ASSESSMENT AND MATH TUTORIALS. The tutorials are designed to familiarize general principles and the self-assessment contains general questions similar to the math questions likely to be on the Accuplacer® exam, but are not intended to be identical to the exam questions. The tutorials are not designed to be a complete math course, and it is assumed that students have some familiarity with math. If you do not understand parts of the tutorial, or find the tutorial difficult, it is recommended that you seek out additional instruction.

Tour of the Accuplacer® Arithmetic Content

The Accuplacer® arithmetic section has 20 questions. Below is a list of the likely arithmetic topics likely to appear on the Accuplacer®. Make sure that you understand these topics at the very minimum.

- Convert decimals, percent, and fractions

- Solve word problems

- Calculate percent and ratio

- Operations using fractions, percent and fractions

- Simple geometry and measurement

- Estimate answers

The questions in the self-assessment are not the same as you will find on the Accuplacer® - that would be too easy! And nobody knows what the questions will be and they change all the time. Mostly, the changes consist of substituting new questions for old, but the changes also can be new question formats or styles, changes to the number of questions in each section, changes to the time limits for each section, and combining sections. So, while the format and exact wording of the questions may differ slightly, and changes from year to year, if you can answer the questions below, you will have no problem with the arithmetic section of the Accuplacer® .

Arithmetic Self-Assessment

The purpose of the self-assessment is:

- Identify your strengths and weaknesses.

- Develop your personalized study plan (above)

- Get accustomed to the Accuplacer® format

- Extra practice – the self-assessments are almost a full 3rd practice test!

- Provide a baseline score for preparing your study schedule.

Since this is a Self-assessment, and depending on how confident you are with arithmetic, timing yourself is optional. The Accuplacer® has 20 questions. This self-assessment has 20 questions, so allow about 20 minutes to complete.

Once complete, use the table below to assess your understanding of the content, and prepare your study schedule described in chapter 1.

80% - 100%	Excellent – you have mastered the content

60 – 79%	Good. You have a working knowledge. Even though you can just pass this section, you may want to review the tutorials and do some extra practice to see if you can improve your mark.
40% - 59%	Below Average. You do not understand basic arithmetic concepts. Review the tutorials , and retake this quiz again in a few days, before proceeding to the practice test questions.
Less than 40%	Poor. You have a very limited understanding of arithmetic. Please review the tutorials , and retake this quiz again in a few days, before proceeding to the practice test questions.

Arithmetic Self-Assessment Answer Sheet

1. Ⓐ Ⓑ Ⓒ Ⓓ   11. Ⓐ Ⓑ Ⓒ Ⓓ

2. Ⓐ Ⓑ Ⓒ Ⓓ   12. Ⓐ Ⓑ Ⓒ Ⓓ

3. Ⓐ Ⓑ Ⓒ Ⓓ   13. Ⓐ Ⓑ Ⓒ Ⓓ

4. Ⓐ Ⓑ Ⓒ Ⓓ   14. Ⓐ Ⓑ Ⓒ Ⓓ

5. Ⓐ Ⓑ Ⓒ Ⓓ   15. Ⓐ Ⓑ Ⓒ Ⓓ

6. Ⓐ Ⓑ Ⓒ Ⓓ   16. Ⓐ Ⓑ Ⓒ Ⓓ

7. Ⓐ Ⓑ Ⓒ Ⓓ   17. Ⓐ Ⓑ Ⓒ Ⓓ

8. Ⓐ Ⓑ Ⓒ Ⓓ   18. Ⓐ Ⓑ Ⓒ Ⓓ

9. Ⓐ Ⓑ Ⓒ Ⓓ   19. Ⓐ Ⓑ Ⓒ Ⓓ

10. Ⓐ Ⓑ Ⓒ Ⓓ   20. Ⓐ Ⓑ Ⓒ Ⓓ

Arithmetic Self-Assessment

1. Brad has agreed to buy everyone a Coke. Each drink costs $1.89, and there are 5 friends. Estimate Brad's cost.

    a. $7

    b. $8

    c. $10

    d. $12

2. Sarah weighs 25 pounds more than Tony. If together they weigh 205 pounds, how much does Sarah weigh approximately in kilograms? Assume 1 pound = 0.4535 kilograms.

    a. 41

    b. 48

    c. 50

    d. 52

3. A building is 15 m long and 20 m wide and 10 m high. What is the volume of the building?

    a. 45 m³

    b. 3,000 m³

    c. 1500 m³

    d. 300 m³

4. 15 is what percent of 200?

    a. 7.5%

    b. 15%

    c. 20%

    d. 17.50%

5. A boy has 5 red balls, 3 white balls and 2 yellow balls. What percent of the balls are yellow?

    a. 2%

    b. 8%

    c. 20%

    d. 12%

6. Add 10% of 300 to 50% of 20

    a. 50

    b. 40

    c. 60

    d. 45

7. Convert 75% to a fraction.

    a. 2/100

    b. 85/100

    c. 3/4

    d. 4/7

8. Multiply 3 by 25% of 40.

    a. 75

    b. 30

    c. 68

    d. 35

9. What is 10% of 30 multiplied by 75% of 200?

    a. 450

    b. 750

    c. 20

    d. 45

10. Convert 4/20 to percent.

    a. 25%

    b. 20%

    c. 40%

    d. 30%

11. Convert 0.55 to percent.

    a. 45%

    b. 15%

    c. 75%

    d. 55%

12. A man buys an item for $420 and has a balance of $3000.00. How much did he have before?

    a. $2,580

    b. $3,420

    c. $2,420

    d. $342

13. What is the best approximate solution for 1.135 - 113.5?

    a. -110

    b. 100

    c. -90

    d. 110

14. Solve 3/4 + 2/4 + 1.2

    a. 1 1/7

    b. 2 3/4

    c. 2 9/20

    d. 3 1/4

15. The average weight of 13 students in a class of 15 (two were absent that day) is 42 kg. When the remaining two are weighed, the average became 42.7 kg. If one of the remaining students weighs 48 kg., how much does the other weigh?

    a. 44.7 kg.

    b. 45.6 kg.

    c. 46.5 kg.

    d. 47.4 kg.

16. The total expense of building a fence around a square-shaped field is $2000 at a rate of $5 per meter. What is the length of one side?

    a. 40 meters

    b. 80 meters

    c. 100 meters

    d. 320 meters

17. There were some oranges in a basket. By adding 8/5 of the total to the basket, the new total is 130. How many oranges were in the basket?

    a. 60

    b. 50

    c. 40

    d. 35

18. 3 boys are asked to clean a surface that is 4 ft^2. If the surface is divided equally among the boys, how much will each clean?

    a. 1 ft 6 inches^2

    b. 14 inches^2

    c. 1 ft 2 inches^2

    d. 1 ft^2 48 inches^2

19. A person earns $25,000 per month and pays $9,000 income tax per year. The Government increased income tax by 0.5% per month and his monthly earning was increased $11,000. How much more income tax will he pay per month?

    a. $1260

    b. $1050

    c. $750

    d. $510

20. Estimate 2009 x 108

    a. 110,000

    b. 2,0000

    c. 21,000

    d. 210,000

Answer Key

1. C
If there are 5 friends and each drink costs $1.89, we can round up to $2 per drink and estimate the total cost at, 5 X $2 = $10.
The actual cost is 5 X $1.89 = $9.45.

2. D
Let us denote Sarah's weight by "x". Then, since she weighs 25 pounds more than Tony, Tony will be x-25. They together weigh 205 pounds which means that the sum of the two representations will be equal to 205:

Sarah : x

Tony : x - 25

x + (x - 25) = 205 ... by arranging this equation we have:

x + x - 25 = 205

2x - 25 = 205 ... we add 25 to each side in order to have x term alone:

2x - 25 + 25 = 205 + 25

2x = 230

x = 230/2

x = 115 pounds → Sarah weighs 115 pounds. Since 1 pound is 0.4535 kilograms, we need to multiply 115 by 0.4535 in order to have her weight in kilograms:

x = 115 • 0.4535 = 52.1525 kilograms → this is equal to 52 when rounded to the nearest whole number.

3. B
Formula for volume of a shape is L x W x H = 15 x 20 x 10 = 3,000 m³

4. A
15/200 = X/100
200X = (15 * 100)

1500/20 Cancel zeroes in the numerator and denominator
15/2 = 7.5%.

Notice that the questions asks, What 15 is what percent of
200? The question does not ask, what is 15% of 200! The
answers are very different.

5. C
Total no. of balls = 10, no. of yellow balls = 2, answer = 2/10
X 100 = 20%.

6. B
10% of 300 = 30 and 50% of 20 = 10 so 30 + 10 = 40.

7. C
75% = 75/100 = 3/4

8. B
25% of 40 = 10 and 10 x 3 = 30

9. A
10% of 30 = 3 and 75% of 200 = 150, 3 X 150 = 450

10. B
4/20 X 100 = 1/5 X 100 = 20%

11. D
0.55 X 100 = 55%

12. B
(Amount Spent) $420 + $3000 (Balance) = $3420

13. A
1.135 -113.5 = -112.37. Best approximate = -110

14. C
3/4 + 2/4 + 1.2, first convert the decimal to fraction, = 3/4
+ 2/4 + 1 1/5 = ¾ + 2/4 + 6/5 = (find common denominator)

(15 + 10 + 24)/20 = 49/20 = 2 9/20

15. C
Total weight of 13 students with average 42 will be = 42•13 =
546 kg.

The total weight of the remaining 2 will be found by subtracting the total weight of 13 students from the total weight of 15 students: 640.5 - 546 = 94.5 kg.

94.5 = the total weight of two students. One of these students weigh 48 kg, so;

The weight of the other will be = 94.5 – 48 = 46.5 kg

16. C
Total expense is $2000 and we are informed that $5 is spent per meter. Combining these two information, we know that the total length of the fence is 2000/5 = 400 meters.

The fence is built around a square shaped field. If one side of the square is "a," the perimeter of the square is "4a". Here, the perimeter is equal to 400 meters. So,

400 = 4a

100 = a → this means that one side of the square is equal to 100 meters

17. B
Let the number of oranges in the basket before additions = x
Then: X + 8x/5 = 130
5x + 8x = 650
650 = 13x
X = 50

18. D
1 foot is equal to 12 inches. So 1 ft² = 12•12 in²

4 ft² = 4•12•12 in² = 576 in²

This amount of surface area is divided equally among 3 boys.

Each boy will clean 576/3 = 192 in²

192 in² = 144 in² + 48 in²; 144 in² = 1 ft²

So, each boy will clean 1 ft² and 48 in²

19. D
The income tax per year is $9,000. So, the income tax per

month is 9,000/12 = $750.

This person earns $25,000 per month and pays $750 income tax. We need to find the rate of the income tax:

Tax rate: 750•100/25,000 = 3%

Government increased this rate by 0.5% so it became 3.5%.

The income of the person per month is increased $11,000 so it became: $25,000 + $11,000 = $36,000.

The new monthly income tax is: 36,000•3.5/100 = $1260.

Amount of increase in tax per month is: $1260 - $750 = $510.

20. D
2009 x 108 = 210,000

Fraction Tips, Tricks and Shortcuts

When you are writing an exam, time is precious, and anything you can do to answer questions faster, is a real advan-
tage. Here are some ideas, shortcuts, tips and tricks that
can speed up answering fraction problems.

Remember that a fraction is just a number which names
a portion of something. For instance, instead of having a
whole pie, a fraction says you have a part of a pie--such as
a half of one or a fourth of one.

Two digits make up a fraction. The digit on top is known
as the numerator. The digit on the bottom is known as the
denominator. To remember which is which, just remember
that "denominator" and "down" both start with a "d." And
the "downstairs" number is the denominator. So for instance, in ½, the numerator is the 1 and the denominator
(or "downstairs") number is the 2.

☐ It's easy to add two fractions if they have the same
denominator. Just add the digits on top and leave
the bottom one the same: $1/10 + 6/10 = 7/10$.

☐ It's the same with subtracting fractions with the
same denominator: $7/10 - 6/10 = 1/10$.

☐ Adding and subtracting fractions with different denominators is a little more complicated. First, you
have to get the problem so that they do have the
same denominators. The easiest way to do this is to
multiply the denominators: For $2/5 + 1/2$ multiply
5 by 2. Now you have a denominator of 10. But now
you have to change the top numbers too. Since you
multiplied the 5 in 2/5 by 2, you also multiply the
2 by 2, to get 4. So the first number is now 4/10.
Since you multiplied the second number times 5, you
also multiply its top number by 5, to get a final fraction of 5/10. Now you can add 5 and 4 together to
get a final sum of 9/10.

☐ Sometimes you'll be asked to reduce a fraction to
its simplest form. This means getting it to where the

only common factor of the numerator and denominator is 1. Think of it this way: Numerators and denominators are brothers that must be treated the same. If you do something to one, you must do it to the other, or it's just not fair. For instance, if you divide your numerator by 2, then you should also divide the denominator by the same. Let's take an example: The fraction 2/10 . This is not reduced to its simplest terms because there is a number that will divide evenly into both: the number 2. We want to make it so that the only number that will divide evenly into both is 1. What can we divide into 2 to get 1? The number 2, of course! Now to be "fair," we have to do the same thing to the denominator: Divide 2 into 10 and you get 5. So our new, reduced fraction is 1/5.

☐ In some ways, multiplying fractions is the easiest of all: Just multiply the two top numbers and then multiply the two bottom numbers. For instance, with this problem:
2/5 X 2/3 you multiply 2 by 2 and get a top number of 4; then multiply 5 by 3 and get a bottom number of 15. Your answer is 4/15.

☐ Dividing fractions is a bit more involved, but still not too hard. You once again multiply, but only AFTER you have turned the second fraction upside-down. To divide ⅞ by ½, turn the ½ into 2/1, then multiply the top numbers and multiply the bottom numbers: ⅞ X 2/1 gives us 14 on top and 8 on the bottom.

Converting Fractions to Decimals

There are a couple of ways to become good at converting fractions to decimals. One -- the one that will make you the fastest in basic math skills -- is to learn some basic fraction facts. It's a good idea, if you're good at memory, to memorize the following:

1/100 is one hundredth, or .01.

1/50 is two hundredths, or .02.

1/25 is one twenty-fifths or four hundredths, or .04.

1/20 is one twentieth or five hundredths, or .05.

1/10 is one tenth, or .1.

1/8 is one eighth, or one hundred twenty-five thousandths, or. 125.

1/5 is one fifth, or two tenths, or .2.

1/4 is one fourth or twenty-five hundredths, or .25.

1/3 is one third or thirty-three hundredths, or .33.

1/2 is one half or five tenths, or .5.

3/4 is three fourths, or seventy-five hundredths, or .75.

Of course, if you're no good at memorization, another good technique for converting a fraction to a decimal is to manipulate it so that the fraction's denominator is 10, 10, 1000, or some other power of 10. Here's an example: We'll start with ¾. What is the first number in the 4 "times table" that you can multiply and get a multiple of 10? Can you multiply 4 by something to get 10? No. Can you multiply it by something to get 100? Yes! 4 X 25 is 100. So let's take that 25 and multiply it by the numerator in our fraction ¾. The numerator is 3, and 3 X 25 is 75. We'll move the decimal in 75 all the way to the left, and we find that ¾ is .75.

We'll do another one: 1/5. Again, we want to find a power of 10 that 5 goes into evenly. Will 5 go into 10? Yes! It goes 2 times. So we'll take that 2 and multiply it by our numerator, 1, and we get 2. We move the decimal in 2 all the way to the left and find that 1/5 is equal to .2.

Converting Fractions to Percent

Working with either fractions or percents can be intimidating enough. But converting from one to the other? That's a genuine nightmare for those who are not math wizards. But really, it doesn't have to be that way. Here are two ways to make it easier and faster to convert a fraction to a percent.

☐ First, you might remember that a fraction is nothing more than a division problem: you're dividing the bottom number into the top number. So for instance, if we start with a fraction 1/10, we are making a division problem with the 10 outside the bracket and the 1 on the inside. As you remember from your lessons on dividing by decimals, since 10 won't go into 1, you add a decimal and make it 10 into 1.0. 10 into 10 goes 1 time, and since it's behind the decimal, it's .1. And how do we say .1? We say "one tenth," which is exactly what we started with: 1/10. So we have a number we can work with now: .1. When we're dealing with percents, though, we're dealing strictly with hundredths (not tenths). You remember from studying decimals that adding a zero to the right of the number on the right side of the decimal does not change the value. Therefore, we can change .1 into .10 and have the same number--except now it's expressed as hundredths. We have 10 hundredths. That's ten out of 100--which is just another way of saying ten percent (ten per hundred or ten out of 100). In other words .1 = .10 = 10 percent. Remember, if you're changing from a decimal to a percent, get rid of the decimal on the left and replace it with a percent mark on the right: 10%. Let's review those steps again: Divide 10 into 1. Since 10 doesn't go into 1, turn 1 into 1.0. Now divide 10 into 1.0. Since 10 goes into 10 1 time, put it there and add your decimal to make it .1. Since a percent is always "hundredths," let's change .1 into .10. Then remove the decimal on the left and replace with a percent sign on the right. The answer is 10%.

☐ If you're doing these conversions on a multiple-choice test, here's an idea that might be even easier and faster. Let's say you have a fraction of 1/8 and you're asked what the percent is. Since we know that "percent" means hundredths, ask yourself what number we can multiply 8 by to get 100. Since there is no number, ask what number gets us close to 100. That number is 12: 8 X 12 = 96. So it gets us a little less than 100. Now, whatever you do to the denominator, you have to do to the numerator. Let's multiply 1 X 12 and we get 12. However, since 96 is a little less than 100, we know that our answer will be a percent a little MORE than 12%. So if your pos-sible answers on the multiple-choice test are these:

a) 8.5%   b) 19%   c)12.5%   d) 25%

then we know the answer is c) 12.5%, because it's a little MORE than the 12 we got in our math problem above.

Another way to look at this, using multiple choice strategy is you know the answer will be "about" 12. Looking at the other options, they are either too large or too small and can be eliminated right away.

This was an easy example to demonstrate, so don't be fooled! You probably won't get such an easy ques-tion on your exam, but the principle holds just the same. By estimating your answer quickly, you can eliminate options immediately and save precious exam time.

Decimal Tips, Tricks and Shortcuts

Converting Decimals to Fractions

One of the most important tricks for correctly converting a decimal to a fraction doesn't involve math at all. It's simply to learn to say the decimal correctly. If you say "point one" or "point 25" for .1 and 25, you'll have more trouble getting the conversion correct. However, if you know that it's called "one tenth" and "twenty-five hundredths," you're on the way to a correct conversion. That's because, if you know your fractions, you know that "one tenth" looks like this: 1/10. And "twenty-five hundredths" looks like this: 25/100.

Even if you have digits before the decimal, such as 3.4, learning how to say the word will help you with the conversion into a fraction. It's not "three point four," it's "three and four tenths." Knowing this, you know that the fraction which looks like "three and four tenths" is 3 4/10.

Of course, your conversion is not complete until you reduce the fraction to its lowest terms: It's not 25/100, but 1/4.

Converting Decimals to Percent

Changing a decimal to a percent is easy if you remember one math formula: multiply by 100. For instance, if you start with .45, you change it to a percent by simply multiplying it by 100. You then wind up with 45. Add the % sign to the end and you get 45%.

That seems easy enough, right? Here think of it this way: You just take out the decimal and stick in a percent sign on the opposite sign. In other words, the decimal on the left is replaced by the % on the right.

It doesn't work quite that easily if the decimal is in the middle of the number. Let's use 3.7 for example. Here, take out the decimal in the middle and replace it with a 0 % at the end. So 3.7 converted to decimal is 370%.

Percent Tips, Tricks and Shortcuts

Percent problems are not nearly as scary as they appear, if you remember this neat trick:

Draw a cross as in:

Portion	Percent
Whole	100

In the upper left, write PORTION. In the bottom left write WHOLE. In the top right, write PERCENT and in the bottom right, write 100. Whatever your problem is, you will leave blank the unknown, and fill in the other four parts. For example, let's suppose your problem is: Find 10% of 50. Since we know the 10% part, we put 10 in the percent corner. Since the whole number in our problem is 50, we put that in the corner marked whole. You always put 100 underneath the percent, so we leave it as is, which leaves only the top left corner blank. This is where we'll put our answer. Now simply multiply the two corner numbers that are NOT 100. Here, it's 10 X 50. That gives us 500. Now multiply this by the remaining corner, or 100, to get a final answer of 5. 5 is the number that goes in the upper-left corner, and is your final solution.

Another hint to remember: Percents are the same thing as hundredths in decimals. So .45 is the same as 45 hundredths or 45 percent.

Converting Percents to Decimals

Percents are simply a specific type of decimals, so it should be no surprise that converting between the two is actually fairly simple. Here are a few tricks and shortcuts to keep in mind:

☐   Remember that percent literally means "per 100" or "for every 100." So when you speak of 30% you're saying 30 for every 100 or the fraction 30/100. In basic math, you learned that fractions that have 10 or 100 as the denominator can easily be turned into a decimal. 30/100 is thirty hundredths, or expressed as a decimal, .30.

☐ Another way to look at it: To convert a percent to a decimal, simply divide the number by 100. So for instance, if the percent is 47%, divide 47 by 100. The result will be .47. Get rid of the % mark and you're done.

☐ Remember that the easiest way of dividing by 100 is by moving your decimal two spots to the left.

Converting Percents to Fractions

Converting percents to fractions is easy. After all, a percent is nothing except a type of fraction; it tells you what part of 100 that you're talking about. Here are some simple ideas for making the conversion from a percent to a fraction:

☐ If the percent is a whole number -- say 34% -- then simply write a fraction with 100 as the denominator (the bottom number). Then put the percentage itself on top. So 34% becomes 34/100.

☐ Now reduce as you would reduce any percent. Here, by dividing 2 into 34 and 2 into 100, you get 17/50.

☐ If your percent is not a whole number -- say 3.4% --then convert it to a decimal expressed as hundredths. 3.4 is the same as 3.40 (or 3 and forty hundredths). Now ask yourself how you would express "three and forty hundredths" as a fraction. It would, of course, be 3 40/100. Reduce this and it becomes 3 2/5.

How to Solve Word Problems

Most students find math word problems difficult. Tackling word problems is much easier if you have a systematic approach which we outline below.

Here is the biggest tip for studying word problems.

Practice regularly and systematically. Sounds simple and easy right? Yes it is, and yes it really does work.

Word problems are a way of thinking and require you to translate a real word problem into mathematical terms.

Some math instructors go so far as to say that learning how to think mathematically is the main reason for teaching word problems.

So what do we mean by Practice regularly and systematically? Studying word problems and math in general requires a logical and mathematical frame of mind. The only way that you can get this is by practicing regularly, which means everyday.

It is critical that you practice word problems everyday for the 5 days before the exam as a bare minimum.

If you practice and miss a day, you have lost the mathematical frame of mind and the benefit of your previous practice is pretty much gone. Anyone who has done any amount of math will agree – you have to practice everyday.

Everything is important. The other critical point about word problems is that all the information given in the problem has some purpose. There is no unnecessary information! Word problems are typically around 50 words in 1 to 3 sentences. If the sometimes complicated relationships are to be explained in that short an explanation, every word has to count. Make sure that you use every piece of information.

Here are 9 simple steps to solve word problems.

Step 1 – Read through the problem at least three times. The first reading should be a quick scan, and the next two readings should be done slowly with a view to finding answers to these important questions:

What does the problem ask? (Usually located towards the end of the problem)

What does the problem imply? (This is usually a point you were asked to remember).

Mark all information, and underline all important words or phrases.

Step 2 – Try to make a pictorial representation of the problem such as a circle and an arrow to show travel. This makes the problem a bit more real and sensible to you.

A favorite word problem is something like, 1 train leaves Station A travelling at 100 km/hr and another train leaves Station B travelling at 60 km/hr. ...

Draw a line, the two stations, and the two trains at either end. This will solidify the situation in your mind.

Step 3 – Use the information you have to make a table with a blank portion to show information you do not know.

Step 4 – Assign a single letter to represent each unknown data in your table. You can write down the unknown that each letter represents so that you do not make the error of assigning answers to the wrong unknown, because a word problem may have multiple unknowns and you will need to create equations for each unknown.

Step 5 – Translate the English terms in the word problem into a mathematical algebraic equation. Remember that the main problem with word problems is that they are not expressed in regular math equations. Your ability to identify correctly the variables and translate the word problem into an equation determines your ability to solve the problem.

Step 6 – Check the equation to see if it looks like regular equations that you are used to seeing and whether it looks sensible. Does the equation appear to represent the information in the question? Take note that you may need to rewrite some formulas needed to solve the word problem equation. For example, word distance problems may need you rewriting the distance formula, which is Distance = Time x Rate. If the word problem requires that you solve for time you will need to use Distance/Rate and Distance/Time to solve for Rate. If you understand the distance word problem you should be able to identify the variable you need to solve for.

Step 7 – Use algebra rules to solve the derived equation. Take note that the laws of equation demands that what is done on this side of the equation has to also be done on the other side. You have to solve the equation so that the unknown ends alone on one side. Where there are multiple unknowns you will need to use elimination or substitution methods to resolve all the equations.

Step 8 – Check your final answers to see if they make sense with the information given in the problem. For example if the word problem involves a discount, the final price should be less or if a product was taxed then the final answer has to cost more.

Step 9 – Cross check your answers by placing the answer or answers in the first equation to replace the unknown or unknowns. If your answer is correct then both side of the equation must equate or equal. If your answer is not correct then you may have derived a wrong equation or solved the equation wrongly. Repeat the necessary steps to correct.

Types of Word Problems

Word problems can be classified into 12 types. Below are examples of each type with a complete solution. Some types of word problems can be solved quickly using multiple choice strategies and some cannot. Always look for ways to estimate the answer and then eliminate options.

1. Age

A girl is 10 years older than her brother. By next year, she will be twice the age of her brother. What are their ages now?

    a. 25, 15
    b. 19, 9
    c. 21, 11
    d. 29, 19

Solution: B

We will assume that the girl's age is "a" and her brother's is "b." This means that based on the information in the first sentence,
a = 10 + b

Next year, she will be twice her brother's age, which gives
a + 1 = 2(b+1)

We need to solve for one unknown factor and then use the answer to solve for the other. To do this we substitute the value of "a" from the first equation into the second equation. This gives

10+b + 1 = 2b + 2
11 + b = 2b + 2
11 – 2 = 2b – b
b= 9

9 = b this means that her brother is 9 years old. Solving for the girl's age in the first equation gives a = 10 + 9. a = 19 the girl is aged 19. So, the girl is aged 19 and the boy is 9

2. Distance or speed

Two boats travel down a river towards the same destination, starting at the same time. One boat is traveling at 52 km/hr, and the other boat at 43 km/hr. How far apart will they be after 40 minutes?

    a. 46.67 km

    b. 19.23 km

    c. 6.0 km

    d. 14.39 km

Solution: C

After 40 minutes, the first boat will have traveled = 52 km/hr x 40 minutes/60 minutes = 34.66 km
After 40 minutes, the second boat will have traveled = 43 km/hr x 40/60 minutes = 28.66 km

Difference between the two boats will be 34.66 km – 28.66 km = 6.04 km.

Multiple Choice Strategy

First estimate the answer. The first boat is travelling 9 km. faster than the second, for 40 minutes, which is 2/3 of an hour. 2/3 of 9 = 6, as a rough guess of the distance apart.

Options A, B and D can be eliminated right away.

3. Ratio

The instructions in a cookbook states that 700 grams of flour must be mixed in 100 ml of water, and 0.90 grams of salt added. A cook however has just 325 grams of flour. What is the quantity of water and salt that he should use?

    a. 0.41 grams and 46.4 ml
    b. 0.45 grams and 49.3 ml
    c. 0.39 grams and 39.8 ml
    d. 0.25 grams and 40.1 ml

Solution: A

The Cookbook states 700 grams of flour, but the cook only has 325. The first step is to determine the percentage of flour he has 325/700 x 100 = 46.4%
That means that 46.4% of all other items must also be used.
46.4% of 100 = 46.4 ml of water
46.4% of 0.90 = 0.41 grams of salt.

Multiple Choice Strategy

The recipe calls for 700 grams of flour but the cook only has 325, which is just less than half, the quantity of water and salt are going to be about half.

Options C and D can be eliminated right away.   Option B is very close so be careful.   Looking closely at option B, it is exactly half, and since 325 is slightly less than half of 700, it can't be correct.
Option A is correct.

4. Percent

An agent received $6,685 as his commission for selling a property. If his commission was 13% of the selling price, how much was the property?

    a. $68,825

    b. $121,850

    c. $49,025

    d. $51,423

Solution: D

Let's assume that the property price is x
That means from the information given, 13% of x = 6,685
Solve for x,
x = 6685 x 100/13 = $51,423

Multiple Choice Strategy

The commission, 13%, is just over 10%, which is easier to work with. Round up $6685 to $6700, and multiple by 10 for an approximate answer. 10 X 6700 = $67,000. You can do this in your head. Option B is much too big and can be eliminated. Option C is too small and can be eliminated. Options A and D are left and good possibilities.

Do the calculations to make the final choice.

5. Sales & Profit

A store owner buys merchandise for $21,045. He transports them for $3,905 and pays his staff $1,450 to stock the merchandise on his shelves. If he does not incur further costs, how much does he need to sell the items to make $5,000 profit?

    a. $32,500

    b. $29,350

    c. $32,400

    d. $31,400

Solution: D

Total cost of the items is $21,045 + $3,905 + $1,450 = $26,400

Total cost is now $26,400 + $5000 profit = $31,400

Multiple Choice Strategy

Round off and add the numbers up in your head quickly. 21,000 + 4,000 + 1500 = 26500. Add in 5000 profit for a total of 31500.

Option B is too small and can be eliminated. Options C and A are too large and can be eliminated.

6. Tax/Income

A woman earns $42,000 per month and pays 5% tax on her monthly income. If the Government increases her monthly taxes by $1,500, what is her income after tax?

    a. $38,400
    b. $36,050
    c. $40,500
    d. $39, 500

Solution: A

Initial tax on income was 5/100 x 42,000 = $2,100
$1,500 was added to the tax to give $2,100 + 1,500 = $3,600
Income after tax left is $42,000 - $3,600 = $38,400

7. Interest

A man invests $3000 in a 2-year term deposit that pays 3% interest per year. How much will he have at the end of the 2-year term?

    a. $5,200
    b. $3,020
    c. $3,182.7
    d. $3,000

Solution: C

This is a compound interest problem. The funds are invested for 2 years and interest is paid yearly, so in the second year, he will earn interest on the interest paid in the first year.

3% interest in the first year = 3/100 x 3,000 = $90
At end of first year, total amount = 3,000 + 90 = $3,090
Second year = 3/100 x 3,090 = 92.7.
At end of second year, total amount = $3090 + $92.7 = $3,182.7

8. Averaging

The average weight of 10 books is 54 grams. 2 more books were added and the average weight became 55.4. If one of the 2 new books added weighed 62.8 g, what is the weight of the other?

    a. 44.7 g
    b. 67.4 g
    c. 62 g
    d. 52 g

Solution: C

Total weight of 10 books with average 54 grams will be=10×54=540 g
Total weight of 12 books with average 55.4 will be=55.4×12=664.8 g
So total weight of the remaining 2 will be= 664.8 – 540 = 124.8 g
If one weighs 62.8, the weight of the other will be= 124.8 g – 62.8 g = 62 g

Multiple Choice Strategy

Averaging problems can be estimated by looking at which direction the average goes. If additional items are added and the average goes up, the new items much be greater than the average. If the average goes down after new items are added, the new items must be less than the average.

Here, the average is 54 grams and 2 books are added which increases the average to 55.4, so the new books must weight more than 54 grams.

Options A and D can be eliminated right away.

9. Probability

A bag contains 15 marbles of various colors. If 3 marbles are white, 5 are red and the rest are black, what is the probability of randomly picking out a black marble from the bag?

    a. 7/15
    b. 3/15
    c. 1/5
    d. 4/15

Solution: A

Total marbles = 15
Number of black marbles = 15 – (3 + 5) = 7
Probability of picking out a black marble = 7/15

10. Two Variables

A company paid a total of $2850 to book for 6 single rooms and 4 double rooms in a hotel for one night. Another company paid $3185 to book for 13 single rooms for one night in the same hotel. What is the cost for single and double rooms in that hotel?

    a. single= $250 and double = $345
    b. single= $254 and double = $350
    c. single = $245 and double = $305
    d. single = $245 and double = $345

Solution: D

We can determine the price of single rooms from the information given of the second company. 13 single rooms = 3185.

One single room = 3185 / 13 = 245
The first company paid for 6 single rooms at $245. 245 x 6 = $1470

Total amount paid for 4 double rooms by first company = $2850 - $1470 = $1380

Cost per double room = 1380 / 4 = $345

11. Simple Geometry

The length of a rectangle is 5 in. more than its width. The perimeter of the rectangle is 26 in. What is the width and length of the rectangle?

    a. width = 6 inches, Length = 9 inches
    b. width = 4 inches, Length = 9 inches
    c. width =4 inches, Length = 5 inches
    d. width = 6 inches, Length = 11 inches

Solution: B

Formula for perimeter of a rectangle is 2(L + W)
p=26, so 2(L+W) = p
The length is 5 inches more than the width, so
2(w+5) + 2w = 26
2w + 10 + 2w = 26
2w + 2w = 26 - 10
4w = 16

W = 16/4 = 4 inches

L is 5 inches more than w, so L = 5 + 4 = 9 inches.

12. Totals and fractions

A basket contains 125 oranges, mangos and apples. If 3/5 of the fruits in the basket are mangos and only 2/5 of the mangos are ripe, how many ripe mangos are there in the basket?

    a. 30

    b. 68

    c. 55

    d. 47

Solution: A
Number of mangos in the basket is 3/5 x 125 = 75
Number of ripe mangos = 2/5 x 75 = 30

Ratios

In mathematics, a ratio is a relationship between two numbers of the same kind[1] (e.g., objects, persons, students, spoonfuls, units of whatever identical dimension), usually expressed as "a to b" or a:b, sometimes expressed arithmetically as a dimensionless quotient of the two[2] which explicitly indicates how many times the first number contains the second (not necessarily an integer).[3] In layman's terms a ratio represents, simply, for every amount of one thing, how much there is of another thing. For example, suppose I have 10 pairs of socks for every pair of shoes then the ratio of shoes:socks would be 1:10 and the ratio of socks:shoes would be 10:1.

Notation and terminology

The ratio of numbers A and B can be expressed as:[4]
the ratio of A to B
A is to B
A:B

A rational number which is the quotient of A divided by B

The numbers A and B are sometimes called terms with A being the antecedent and B being the consequent.

The proportion expressing the equality of the ratios A:B and C:D is written A:B=C:D or A:B::C:D. This form, when spoken or written in the English language, is often expressed as A is to B as C is to D.

Again, A, B, C, D are called the terms of the proportion. A and D are called the extremes, and B and C are called the means. The equality of three or more proportions is called a continued proportion.[5]
Ratios are sometimes used with three or more terms. The dimensions of a two by four that is ten inches long are 2:4:10.

Examples

The quantities being compared in a ratio might be physical quantities such as speed or length, or numbers of objects, or amounts of particular substances. A common example of the last case is the weight ratio of water to cement used in concrete, which is commonly stated as 1:4. This means that the weight of cement used is four times the weight of water used. It does not say anything about the total amounts of cement and water used, nor the quantity of concrete being made. Equivalently it could be said that the ratio of cement to water is 4:1, that there is 4 times as much cement as water, or that there is a quarter (1/4) as much water as cement..
Older televisions have a 4:3 "aspect ratio," which means that the width is 4/3 of the height; modern widescreen TVs have a 16:9 aspect ratio.

Fractional

If there are 2 oranges and 3 apples, the ratio of oranges to apples is 2:3, and the ratio of oranges to the total number of pieces of fruit is 2:5. These ratios can also be expressed in fraction form: there are 2/3 as many oranges as apples, and 2/5 of the pieces of fruit are oranges. If orange juice concentrate is to be diluted with water in the ratio 1:4, then one part of concentrate is mixed with four parts of water, giving five parts total; the quantity of orange juice concentrate is

1/4 the amount of water, while the amount of orange juice concentrate is 1/5 of the total liquid. In both ratios and fractions, it is important to be clear what is being compared to what, and beginners often make mistakes for this reason.

Number of terms

In general, when comparing the quantities of a two-quantity ratio, this can be expressed as a fraction derived from the ratio. For example, in a ratio of 2:3, the amount/size/volume/number of the first quantity will be that of the second quantity. This pattern also works with ratios with more than two terms. However, a ratio with more than two terms cannot be completely converted into a single fraction; a single fraction represents only one part of the ratio since a fraction can only compare two numbers. If the ratio deals with objects or amounts of objects, this is often expressed as "for every two parts of the first quantity there are three parts of the second quantity."

Percent and ratio

If we multiply all quantities involved in a ratio by the same number, the ratio remains valid. For example, a ratio of 3:2 is the same as 12:8. It is usual either to reduce terms to the lowest common denominator, or to express them in parts per hundred (percent).

If a mixture contains substances A, B, C & D in the ratio 5:9:4:2 then there are 5 parts of A for every 9 parts of B, 4 parts of C and 2 parts of D. As 5+9+4+2=20, the total mixture contains 5/20 of A (5 parts out of 20), 9/20 of B, 4/20 of C, and 2/20 of D. If we divide all numbers by the total and multiply by 100, this is converted to percentages: 25% A, 45% B, 20% C, and 10% D (equivalent to writing the ratio as 25:45:20:10).

Proportion

If the two or more ratio quantities encompass all the quantities in a particular situation, for example two apples and three oranges in a fruit basket containing no other types of fruit, it could be said that "the whole" contains five parts, made up of two parts apples and three parts oranges. Here, or 40% of the whole are apples or 60% of the whole are oranges. This comparison of a specific quantity to "the whole" is sometimes called a proportion. Proportions are sometimes expressed as percentages as demonstrated above.

Reduction

Note that ratios can be reduced (as fractions are) by dividing each quantity by the common factors of all the quantities. This is often called "cancelling." As for fractions, the simplest form is considered to be that in which the numbers in the ratio are the smallest possible integers.

Thus, the ratio 40:60 may be considered equivalent in meaning to the ratio 2:3 within contexts concerned only with relative quantities.

Mathematically, we write: "40:60" = "2:3" (dividing both quantities by 20).
Grammatically, we would say, "40 to 60 equals 2 to 3."
An alternative representation is: "40:60::2:3"
Grammatically, we would say, "40 is to 60 as 2 is to 3."
A ratio that has integers for both quantities and that cannot be reduced any further (using integers) is said to be in simplest form or lowest terms.
Sometimes it is useful to write a ratio in the form 1:n or n:1 to enable comparisons of different ratios.

For example, the ratio 4:5 can be written as 1:1.25 (dividing both sides by 4). Alternately, 4:5 can be written as 0.8:1 (dividing both sides by 5). Where the context makes the meaning clear, a ratio in this form is sometimes written without the 1 and the colon, though, mathematically, this makes it a factor or multiplier. [11]

Algebra

THIS SECTION CONTAINS A SELF-ASSESSMENT AND ALGEBRA TU-
TORIALS. The tutorials are designed to familiarize general principles and the self-assessment contains general
questions similar to the algebra questions likely to be on the
Accuplacer® exam, but are not intended to be identical to the
exam questions. The tutorials are not designed to be a complete algebra course, and it is assumed that students have
some familiarity with algebra. If you do not understand parts
of the tutorial, or find the tutorial difficult, it is recommended
that you seek out additional instruction.

Tour of the Accuplacer® Algebra Content

The Accuplacer® algebra section has 20 questions. Below
is a list of the likely algebra topics likely to appear on the
Accuplacer®. Make sure that you understand these topics at
the very minimum.

- Operations with polynomials

- Exponents

- Solving Inequalities

- Linear equations with one and two variables

- Solving quadratics

The questions in the self-assessment are not the same as
you will find on the Accuplacer® - that would be too easy!
And nobody knows what the questions will be and they

change all the time. Mostly, the changes consist of sub-stituting new questions for old, but the changes also can be new question formats or styles, changes to the number of questions in each section, changes to the time limits for each section, and combining sections. So, while the format and exact wording of the questions may differ slightly, and changes from year to year, if you can answer the questions below, you will have no problem with the algebra section of the Accuplacer®.

Algebra Self-Assessment

The purpose of the self-assessment is:

*   Identify your strengths and weaknesses.

*   Develop your personalized study plan (above)

*   Get accustomed to the Accuplacer® format

*   Extra practice – the self-assessments are almost a full 3rd practice test!

*   Provide a baseline score for preparing your study schedule.

Since this is a Self-assessment, and depending on how con-fident you are with algebra, timing yourself is optional. The Accuplacer® has 20 questions. This self-assessment has 17 questions, so allow about 20 minutes to complete.

Once complete, use the table below to assess your under-standing of the content, and prepare your study schedule described in chapter 1.

80% - 100%	Excellent – you have mastered the content

60 – 79%	Good. You have a working knowledge. Even though you can just pass this section, you may want to review the tutorials and do some extra practice to see if you can improve your mark.
40% - 59%	Below Average. You do not understand algebra. Review the tutorials , and retake this quiz again in a few days, before proceeding to the practice test questions.
Less than 40%	Poor. You have a very limited understanding of algebra. Please review the tutorials , and retake this quiz again in a few days, before proceeding to the practice test questions.

Algebra Self-Assessment Answer Sheet

1. (A) (B) (C) (D)   11. (A) (B) (C) (D)

2. (A) (B) (C) (D)   12. (A) (B) (C) (D)

3. (A) (B) (C) (D)   13. (A) (B) (C) (D)

4. (A) (B) (C) (D)   14. (A) (B) (C) (D)

5. (A) (B) (C) (D)   15. (A) (B) (C) (D)

6. (A) (B) (C) (D)   16. (A) (B) (C) (D)

7. (A) (B) (C) (D)   17. (A) (B) (C) (D)

8. (A) (B) (C) (D)

9. (A) (B) (C) (D)

10. (A) (B) (C) (D)

Exponents

1. Express in 3^4 standard form

    a. 81

    b. 27

    c. 12

    d. 9

2. Simplify $4^3 + 2^4$

    a. 45

    b. 108

    c. 80

    d. 48

3. If $x = 2$ and $y = 5$, solve $xy^3 - x^3$

    a. 240

    b. 258

    c. 248

    d. 242

4. $X^3 \times X^2 =$

    a. 5^x

    b. x^{-5}

    c. x^{-1}

    d. X^5

5. Express 100000⁰ in standard form.

    a. 1

    b. 0

    c. 100000

    d. 1000

6. Solve √144

    a. 14

    b. 72

    c. 24

    d. 12

Linear Equations

7. Solve the linear equation: -x - 7 = -3x - 9

    a. -1

    b. 0

    c. 1

    d. 2

8. Solve the system: 4x - y = 5   x + 2y = 8

    a. (3,2)

    b. (3,3)

    c. (2,3)

    d. (2,2)

Polynomials

9. Add -3x² + 2x + 6 and -x² - x - 1.

  a. $-2x^2 + x + 5$
  b. $-4x^2 + x + 5$
  c. $-2x^2 + 3x + 5$
  d. $-4x^2 + 3x + 5$

10. Simplify the following expression:

3x³ + 2x² + 5x - 7 + 4x² - 5x + 2 - 3x³

  a. $6x^2 - 9$
  b. $6x^2 - 5$
  c. $6x^2 - 10x - 5$
  d. $6x^2 + 10x - 9$

11. Multiply x - 1 and x² + x + 2.

  a. $x^3 + x - 2$
  b. $x^2 + x - 2$
  c. $x^3 + x^2 - 2$
  d. $x^3 + 2x^2 - 2$

12. Factor the polynomial 9x² - 6x + 12.

  a. $3(x^2 - 2x + 9)$
  b. $3(3x^2 - 3x + 4)$
  c. $9(x^2 - 3x + 3)$
  d. $3(3x^2 - 2x + 4)$

Quadratics

13. Find 2 numbers that sum to 21 and the sum of the squares is 261.

      a. 14 and 7

      b. 15 and 6

      c. 16 and 5

      d. 17 and 4

14. Using the factoring method, solve the quadratic equation: $x^2 + 4x + 4 = 0$

      a. 0 and 1

      b. 1 and 2

      c. 2

      d. -2

15. Using the quadratic formula, solve the quadratic equation: $x - 31/x = 0$

      a. $-\sqrt{13}$ and $\sqrt{13}$
      b. $-\sqrt{31}$ and $\sqrt{31}$
      c. $-\sqrt{31}$ and $2\sqrt{31}$
      d. $-\sqrt{3}$ and $\sqrt{3}$

16. Using the factoring method, solve the quadratic equation: $2x^2 - 3x = 0$

      a. 0 and 1.5

      b. 1.5 and 2

      c. 2 and 2.5

      d. 0 and 2

17. Using the quadratic formula, solve the quadratic equation: $x^2 - 9x + 14 = 0$

    a. 2 and 7

    b. -2 and 7

    c. -7 and -2

    d. -7 and 2

Answer Key

Exponents

1. A
3 x 3 x 3 x 3 = 81

2. C
(4 x 4 x 4) + (2 x 2 x 2 x 2) = 64 + 16 = 80

3. D
$2(5)^3 - (2)^3 = 2(125) - 8 = 250 - 8 = 242$

4. D
$X^3 \times X^2 = X^{3+2} = X^5$
To multiply exponents with like bases, add the exponents.

5. A
Any value (except 0) raised to the power of 0 equals 1.

6. D
$\sqrt{144} = 12$

Linear Equations

7. A
We should collect similar terms on the same side. Here, we can collect x terms on left side, and the constants on the right side:

- x - 7 = - 3x - 9 .... Let us add 3x to both sides:

- x - 7 + 3x = - 3x - 9 + 3x

2x - 7 = - 9 ... Now, we can add + 7 to both sides:

2x - 7 + 7 = - 9 + 7

2x = - 2 ... Dividing both sides by 2 gives us the value of x:

x = -2/2

x = -1

8. C

First, we need to write two equations separately:

4x - y = 5 (I)

x + 2y = 8 (II) ... Here, we can use two ways to solve the system. One is substitution method, the other one is linear elimination method:

Method 1 - Substitution Method

Equation (I) gives us that y = 4x - 5. We insert this value of y into equation (II):

x + 2(4x - 5) = 8

x + 8x - 10 = 8

9x - 10 = 8

9x = 18

x = 2

Bu knowing x = 2, we can find the value of y by inserting x = 2 into either of the equations. Let us choose equation (I):

4(2) - y = 5

8 - y = 5

8 - 5 = y

y = 3 → solution is (2, 3)

Method 2 - Linear Elimination Method

2•/ 4x - y = 5 ... by multiplying equation (I) by 2, we see that -2y will form; and y terms

    x + 2y = 8 ... will be eliminated when summed with +2y in equation (II):

2•/ 4x - y = 5

+   x + 2y = 8

    8x - 2y = 10

+   x + 2y = 8 ... Summing side by side:

8x + x - 2y + 2y = 10 + 8 ... -2y and +2y eliminate each
    other:

9x = 18

x = 2

By knowing x = 2, we can find the value of y by inserting x =
2 into either of the equations. Let us choose equation (I):

4(2) - y = 5

8 - y = 5

8 - 5 = y

y = 3 → solution is (2, 3)

Polynomials

9. B
$(-3x^2 + 2x + 6) + (-x^2 - x - 1)$

$= -3x^2 + 2x + 6 - x^2 - x - 1$ ... we write similar terms together:

$= -3x^2 - x^2 + 2x - x + 6 - 1$ ... we operate within the same
terms:

$= -4x^2 + x + 5$

10. B
$3x^3 + 2x^2 + 5x - 7 + 4x^2 - 5x + 2 - 3x^3$ ... we write similar
terms together:

$= 3x^3 - 3x^3 + 2x^2 + 4x^2 + 5x - 5x - 7 + 2$ ... we operate within
the same terms. $3x^3$ and $- 3x^3$, 5x and -5x cancel each other:

$= 6x^2 - 5$

11. A
We are asked to multiply $(x - 1)(x^2 + x + 2)$.

Each term in the parenthesis (x - 1) should be multiplied to each term in the parenthesis $(x^2 + x + 2)$:

$= x(x^2 + x + 2) - 1(x^2 + x + 2) = x^3 + x^2 + 2x - x^2 - x - 2$ ... we write similar terms together:

$= x^3 + x^2 - x^2 + 2x - x - 2$ ... we operate within the same terms. x^2 and $-x^2$ cancel each other:

$= x^3 + x - 2$

12. D
First, we need to search for a constant common factor in each of the terms. If there is any, we need to take it out of the equation and write it as a coefficient in front:

$9x^2 - 6x + 12 = 3(3x^2 - 2x + 4)$

We cannot go further from this point, so this is the factored form of the polynomial.

Quadratics

13. B
There are two statements made. This means that we can write two equations according to these statements:
The sum of two numbers are 21: $x + y = 21$

The sum of the squares is 261: $x^2 + y^2 = 261$

We are asked to find x and y.

Since we have the sums of the numbers and the sums of their squares; we can use the square formula of x + y, that is:

$(x + y)^2 = x^2 + 2xy + y^2$ ... Here, we can insert the known values x + y and $x^2 + y^2$:

$(21)^2 = 261 + 2xy$ ... Arranging to find xy:

$441 = 261 + 2xy$

$441 - 261 = 2xy$

$180 = 2xy$

xy = 180/2

xy = 90

We need to find two number which multiply to 90. Checking the answer choices, we see that in (b), 15 and 6 are given. $15 \cdot 6 = 90$. Also their squares sum up to 261 ($15^2 + 6^2 = 225 + 36 = 261$). So these two numbers satisfy the equation.

14. D
$x^2 + 4x + 4 = 0$ ... We try to separate the middle term 4x to find common factors with x^2 and 4 separately:

$x^2 + 2x + 2x + 4 = 0$ ... Here, we see that x is a common factor for x^2 and 2x, and 2 is a common factor for 2x and 4:

x(x + 2) + 2(x + 2) = 0 ... Here, we have x times x + 2 and 2 times x + 2 summed up. This means that we have x + 2 times x + 2:

(x + 2)(x + 2) = 0

$(x + 2)^2 = 0$ ... This is true if only if x + 2 is equal to zero.

x + 2 = 0

x = -2

15. B
To solve the equation, first we need to arrange it to appear in the form $ax^2 + bx + c = 0$ by removing the denominator:

x - 31/x = 0 ... First, we enlarge the equation by x:

$x \cdot x - 31 \cdot x/x = 0$

$x^2 - 31 = 0$

The quadratic formula to find the roots of a quadratic equation is:

$x_{1,2} = (-b \pm \sqrt{\Delta}) / 2a$ where $\Delta = b^2 - 4ac$ and is called the discriminant of the quadratic equation.

In our question, the equation is $x^2 - 31 = 0$. By remembering the form $ax^2 + bx + c = 0$:

a = 1, b = 0, c = -31

So, we can find the discriminant first, and then the roots of the equation:

$\Delta = b^2 - 4ac = 0^2 - 4 \cdot 1 \cdot (-31) = 124$

$x_{1,2} = (-b \pm \sqrt{\Delta}) / 2a = (\pm \sqrt{124}) / 2 = (\pm \sqrt{4 \cdot 31}) / 2 = (\pm 2\sqrt{31}) / 2$
... Simplifying by 2:

$x_{1,2} = \pm\sqrt{31}$ ... This means that the roots are $\sqrt{31}$ and $-\sqrt{31}$.

16. A
$2x^2 - 3x = 0$ ... we see that both of the terms contain x; so we can take it out as a factor:

$x(2x - 3) = 0$ ... two terms are multiplied and the result is zero. This means that either of the terms or both of the terms can be equal to zero:

$x = 0$ ... this is one solution

$2x - 3 = 0 \rightarrow 2x = 3 \rightarrow x = 3/2 \rightarrow x = 1.5$ ... this is the second solution.

So, the solutions are 0 and 1.5.

17. A
To solve the equation, we need the equation in the form $ax^2 + bx + c = 0$.

$x^2 - 9x + 14 = 0$ is already in this form.

The quadratic formula to find the roots of a quadratic equation is:

$x_{1,2} = (-b \pm \sqrt{\Delta}) / 2a$ where $\Delta = b^2 - 4ac$ and is called the discriminant of the quadratic equation.

In our question, the equation is $x^2 - 9x + 14 = 0$. By remembering the form $ax^2 + bx + c = 0$:

$a = 1, b = -9, c = 14$

So, we can find the discriminant first, and then the roots of the equation:

$\Delta = b^2 - 4ac = (-9)^2 - 4 \cdot 1 \cdot 14 = 81 - 56 = 25$

$x_{1,2} = (-b \pm \sqrt{\Delta}) / 2a = (-(-9) \pm \sqrt{25}) / 2 = (9 \pm 5) / 2$

This means that the roots are,

$x_1 = (9 - 5) / 2 = 2$ and $x_2 = (9 + 5) / 2 = 7$

Exponents: Tips, Shortcuts & Tricks

Exponents seem like advanced math to most—like some mysterious code with a complicated meaning. In fact, though, an exponent is just short hand for saying that you're multiplying a number by itself two or more times. For instance, instead of saying that you're multiplying 5 x 5 x 5, you can show that you're multiplying 5 by itself 3 times if you just write 5^3. We usually say this as "five to the third power" or "five to the power of three." In this example, the raised 3 is an "exponent," while the 5 is the "base." You can even use exponents with fractions. For instance, $1/2^3$ means you're multiplying $1/2$ x $1/2$ x $1/2$. (The answer is $1/8$). Some other helpful hints for working with exponents:

- Here's how to do basic multiplication of exponents. If you have the same number with a different exponent (For instance 5^3 X 5^2) just add the exponents and multiply the bases as usual. The answer, then, is 25^5.
- This doesn't work, though, if the bases are different. For instance, in 5^3 X 3^2 we simply have to do the math the long way to figure out the final solution: 5 x 5 x 5, multiplying that result times the result for 3 X 3. (The answer is 1125).
- Looking at it from the opposite side, to divide two exponents with the same base (or bottom number), subtract the smaller exponent from the larger one. If we were dividing the problem above, we would subtract the 2 from the 3 to get 1. 5 to the power of 1 is simply 5.
- One time when thinking of exponents as merely multiplication doesn't work is when the raised number is zero. Any number raised to the "zeroth" power is 1 (Not, as we tend to think, zero).

Number (x)	X^2	X^3
1	1	1
2	4	8
3	9	27
4	16	64
5	25	125
6	36	216
7	49	343
8	64	512
9	81	729
10	100	1000
11	121	1331
12	144	1728
13	169	2197
14	196	2744
15	225	3375
16	256	4096

Solving One-Variable Linear Equations

Linear equations with variable x is an equation with the following form:

$$ax = b$$

where a and b are real numbers. If a=0 and b is different from 0, then the equation has no solution.

Let's solve one simple example of a linear equation with one variable:

$$4x - 2 = 2x + 6$$

When we are given this type of equation, we are always moving variables to the one side, and real numbers to the other side of the equals sign. Always remember: if you are changing sides, you are changing signs. Let's move all variables to the left, and real number to the right side:

4x - 2 = 2x + 6
4x - 2x = 6 + 2
2x = 8
x = 8/2
x = 4

When 2x goes to the left it becomes -2x, and -2 goes to the right and becomes +2. After calculations, we find that x is 4, which is a solution of our linear equation.

Let's solve a little more complex linear equation:

2x - 6/4 + 4 = x
2x - 6 + 16 = 4x
2x - 4x = -16 + 6
-2x = -10
x = -10/-2
x = 5

We multiply whole equation by 4, to lose the fractional line. Now we have a simple linear equation. If we change sides, we change the signs.

Solving Two-Variable Linear Equations

If we have 2 or more linear equations with 2 or more variables, then we have a system of linear equations. The idea here is to express one variable using the other in one equation, and then use it in the second equation, so we get a linear equation with one variable. Here is an example:
x - y = 3
2x + y = 9

From the first equation, we express y using x.

y = x - 3

In the second equation, we write x-3 instead of y. And there we get a linear equation with one variable x.

2x + x - 3 = 9
3x = 9 + 3
3x = 12
x = 12/3
x = 4

Now that we found x, we can use it to find y.

y = x - 3
y = 4 - 3
y = 1

So, the solution of this system is (x,y) = (4,1).

Let's solve one more system using a different method:

Solve:

5x - 3y = 17
x + 3y = 11

5x - 3y + x + 3y = 17 - 11

Notice that we have -3y in the first equation and +3y in the second. If we add these 2, we get zero, which means we lose variable y. So, we add these 2 equations and we get a linear equation with one variable.

6x = 6
x = 1

Now that we have x, we use it to find y.

5 - 3y = 17
-3y = 17 - 5
-3y = 12

y = 12/(-3)
y = -4

Adding and Subtracting Polynomials

When we are adding or subtracting 2 or more polynomials, we have to first group the same variables (arguments) that have the same degrees and then add or subtract them. For example, if we have ax^3 in one polynomial (where a is some real number), we have to group it with bx^3 from the other polynomial (where b is also some real number). Here is one example with adding polynomials:

$(-x^2 + 2x + 3) + (2x^2 + 4x - 5) =$
$-x^2 + 2x + 3 + 2x^2 + 4x - 5 =$
$x^2 + 6x - 2$

We remove the brackets, and since we have a plus in front of every bracket, the signs in the polynomials don't change. We group variables with the same degrees. We have -1 + 2, which is 1 and that's how we got x^2. For the first degree, where we have 2 + 4 which is 6, and the constants (real numbers) where we have 3 - 5 which is -2.

The principle is the same with subtracting, only we have to keep in mind that a minus in front of the polynomial changes all signs in that polynomial. Here is one example:

$(4x^3 - x^2 + 3) - (-3x^2 - 10) =$
$4x^3 - x^2 + 3 + 3x^2 + 10 =$
$4x^3 + 2x^2 + 13$

We remove the brackets, and since we have a minus in front of the second polynomial, all signs in that polynomial change. We have $-3x^2$ and with minus in front, it becomes a plus and same goes for -10.

Now we group the variables with same degrees: there is no variable with the third degree in the second polynomial, so we just write $4x^3$. We group other variables the same way as adding polynomials.

Multiplying and Dividing Polynomials

If we have two polynomials that we need to multiply, then multiply each member of the first polynomial with each member of the second. Let's see in one example how this works:

$(x-1)(x-2) = x^2 - 2x - x + 2 = x^2 - 3x + 2$

The first member of the first polynomial is multiplied with the first member of the second polynomial and then with the second member of the second polynomial. Continue the process with the second member of the first polynomial, then simplify.

To multiply more polynomials, multiply the first 2, then multiply that result with next polynomial and so on. Here is one example:

$(1 - x)(2 - x)(3 - x) = (2 - x - 2x + x^2)(3-x)$
$= (2 - 3x + x^2)(3 - x)$
$= 6 - 2x - 9x + 3x^2 + 3x^2 - x^3 = 6 - 11x + 6x^2 - x^3$

Simplifying Polynomials

Let's say we are given some expression with one or more variables, where we have to add, subtract and multiply polynomials. We do the calculations with variables and constants and then we group the variables with the appropriate degrees. As a result, we would get a polynomial. This process is called simplifying polynomials, where we go from a complex expression to a simple polynomial.

Example:

Simplify the following expression and arrange the degrees from bigger to smaller:

$4 + 3x - 2x^2 + 5x + 6x^3 - 2x^2 + 1 = 6x^3 - 4x^2 + 8x + 5$

We can have more complex expressions such as:

$(x + 5)(1 - x) - (2x - 2) = x - x^2 + 5 - 5x - 2x + 2 = -x^2 - 6x + 7$

Here, first we multiply the polynomials and then we subtract the result and the third polynomial.

Factoring Polynomials

If we have a polynomial that we want to write as multiplication of a real number and a polynomial or as a multiplication of 2 or more polynomials, then we are dealing with factoring polynomials.

Let's see an example for a simple factoring:

$12x^2 + 6x - 4 =$
$2 * 6x^2 + 2 * 3x - 2 * 2 =$
$2(6x^2 + 3x - 2)$

We look at every polynomial member as a product of a real number and a variable. Notice that all real numbers in the polynomial are even, so they have the same number (factor). We pull out that 2 in front of the polynomial, and we write what is left.

What if have a more complex case, where we can't find a factor that is a real number? Here is an example:

$x^2 - 2x + 1 =$
$x^2 - x - x + 1 =$
$x(x - 1) - (x - 1) =$
$(x - 1)(x - 1)$

We can write $-2x$ as $-x-x$. Now we group first 2 members and we see that they have the same factor x, which we can pull in front of them. For the other 2 members, we pull the minus in front of them, so we can get the same binomial that we got with the first 2 members. Now we have that this binomial is the factor for x(x-1) and (x-1).

If we pull x-1 in front (underlined), from the first member we are left with x, and from the second we have -1.

And that is how we transform a polynomial into a product of 2 polynomials (in this case binomials).

Quadratic equations

A. Factoring

Quadratic equations are usually called second degree equations, which mean that the second degree is the highest degree of the variable that can be found in the quadratic equation. The form of these equations is:

$$ax^2 + bx + c = 0$$

where a, b and c are some real numbers.

One way for solving quadratic equations is the factoring method, where we transform the quadratic equation into a product of 2 or more polynomials. Let's see how that works in one simple example:

$$x^2 + 2x = 0$$

$$x(x+2) = 0$$

$$(x = 0) \vee (x + 2 = 0)$$

$$(x = 0) \vee (x = -2)$$

Notice that here we don't have parameter c, but this is still a quadratic equation, because we have the second degree of variable x. Our factor here is x, which we put in front, and we are left with x+2. The equation is equal to 0, so either x or x+2 are 0, or, both are 0.

So, our 2 solutions are 0 and -2.

B. Quadratic formula

If we are unsure how to rewrite quadratic equations so we can solve it using factoring method, we can use the formula for quadratic equation:

$$x_{1,2} = \frac{-b \pm \sqrt{b^2 - 4ac}}{2a}$$

We write $x_{1,2}$ because it represents 2 solutions of the equation. Here is one example:

$$3x^2 - 10x + 3 = 0$$

$$x_{1,2} = \frac{-b \pm \sqrt{b^2 - 4ac}}{2a}$$

$$x_{1,2} = \frac{-(-10) \pm \sqrt{(-10)^2 - 4 \cdot 3 \cdot 3}}{2 \cdot 3}$$

$$x_{1,2} = \frac{10 \pm \sqrt{100 - 36}}{6}$$

$$x_{1,2} = \frac{10 \pm \sqrt{64}}{6}$$

$$x_{1,2} = \frac{10 \pm 8}{6}$$

$$x_1 = \frac{10 + 8}{6} = \frac{18}{6} = 3$$

$$x_2 = \frac{10 - 8}{6} = \frac{2}{6} = \frac{1}{3}$$

We see that a is 3, b is -10 and c is 3.
We use these numbers in the equation and do some calculations.

Notice that we have + and -, so x_1 is for + and x_2 is for -, and that's how we get 2 solutions.

College Level Math

T HIS SECTION CONTAINS A SELF-ASSESSMENT AND COLLEGE LEVEL MATH TUTORIALS. The tutorials are designed to familiarize general principles and the self-assessment contains general questions similar to the college level math questions likely to be on the Accuplacer® exam, but are not intended to be identical to the exam questions. The tutorials are not designed to be a complete course, and it is assumed that students have some familiarity with college level math. If you do not understand parts of the tutorial, or find the tutorial difficult, it is recommended that you seek out additional instruction.

Tour of the Accuplacer® College Level Math Content

The Accuplacer® college level math section has 20 questions. Below is a list of the likely college level math topics likely to appear on the Accuplacer®. Make sure that you understand these topics at the very minimum.

- Coordinate geometry

- Trigonometry

- Solutions of inequalities

- Logarithms

- Sequences

The questions in the self-assessment are not the same as

you will find on the Accuplacer® - that would be too easy! And nobody knows what the questions will be and they change all the time. Mostly, the changes consist of substituting new questions for old, but the changes also can be new question formats or styles, changes to the number of questions in each section, changes to the time limits for each section, and combining sections. So, while the format and exact wording of the questions may differ slightly, and changes from year to year, if you can answer the questions below, you will have no problem with the college level math section of the Accuplacer®.

College level math Self-Assessment

The purpose of the self-assessment is:

- Identify your strengths and weaknesses.

- Develop your personalized study plan (above)

- Get accustomed to the Accuplacer® format

- Extra practice – the self-assessments are almost a full 3rd practice test!

- Provide a baseline score for preparing your study schedule.

Since this is a Self-assessment, and depending on how confident you are with college level math, timing yourself is optional. The Accuplacer® has 20 questions. This self-assessment has 20 questions, so allow about 20 minutes to complete.

Once complete, use the table below to assess your understanding of the content, and prepare your study schedule described in chapter 1.

80% - 100%	Excellent – you have mastered the content
60 – 79%	Good. You have a working knowledge. Even though you can just pass this section, you may want to review the tutorials and do some extra practice to see if you can improve your mark.
40% - 59%	Below Average. You do not understand college level math. Review the tutorials , and retake this quiz again in a few days, before proceeding to the practice test questions.
Less than 40%	Poor. You have a very limited understanding of college level math. Please review the tutorials , and retake this quiz again in a few days, before proceeding to the practice test questions.

Answer Sheet

1. Ⓐ Ⓑ Ⓒ Ⓓ   11. Ⓐ Ⓑ Ⓒ Ⓓ

2. Ⓐ Ⓑ Ⓒ Ⓓ   12. Ⓐ Ⓑ Ⓒ Ⓓ

3. Ⓐ Ⓑ Ⓒ Ⓓ   13. Ⓐ Ⓑ Ⓒ Ⓓ

4. Ⓐ Ⓑ Ⓒ Ⓓ   14. Ⓐ Ⓑ Ⓒ Ⓓ

5. Ⓐ Ⓑ Ⓒ Ⓓ   15. Ⓐ Ⓑ Ⓒ Ⓓ

6. Ⓐ Ⓑ Ⓒ Ⓓ   16. Ⓐ Ⓑ Ⓒ Ⓓ

7. Ⓐ Ⓑ Ⓒ Ⓓ   17. Ⓐ Ⓑ Ⓒ Ⓓ

8. Ⓐ Ⓑ Ⓒ Ⓓ   18. Ⓐ Ⓑ Ⓒ Ⓓ

9. Ⓐ Ⓑ Ⓒ Ⓓ   19. Ⓐ Ⓑ Ⓒ Ⓓ

10. Ⓐ Ⓑ Ⓒ Ⓓ   20. Ⓐ Ⓑ Ⓒ Ⓓ

Geometry

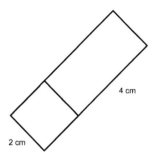

Note: Figure not drawn to scale

1. Assuming the shape with 2 cm side is square, what is the perimeter of the above shape?

    a.   12 cm
    b.   16 cm
    c.   6 cm
    d.   20 cm

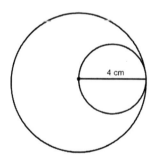

Note: Figure not drawn to scale

2. Assuming the diameter of the small circle is equal to the radius of the large circle, what is (area of large circle) - (area of small circle) in the figure above?

    a. 8π cm^2
    b. 10π cm^2
    c. 12π cm^2
    d. 16π cm^2

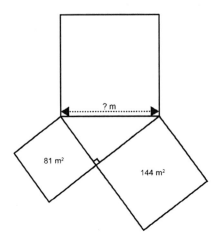

Note: Figure not drawn to scale

3. Assuming the shapes around the right triangle are square, what is the length of each side of the indicated square above?

 a. 10
 b. 15
 c. 20
 d. 5

Trigonometry

4. If sides a and b of a right triangle are 8 and 6, respectively, find cosine of a.

 a. 1/5
 b. 5/3
 c. 3/5
 d. 2/5

5. Find tangent of a of a right triangle, if a is 3 and b is 5.

    a. 1/4

    b. 5/3

    c. 1

    d. 3/5

6. If a=300, find sin30° + cos60°.

    a. 1/2

    b. 2/3

    c. 1

    d. 3/2

Inequalities

7. Solve the inequality: -7x - 1 ≥ 13

    a. $[2, + \infty)$

    b. $(7, + \infty)$

    c. $(-\infty, -2]$

    d. $[2, + \infty)$

8. Solve the inequality: 2x - 1 ≥ x + 10

    a. $(-\infty, 9)$

    b. $[9, +\infty)$

    c. $(-\infty, -9)$

    d. $[11, +\infty)$

Logarithms

9. If $\log_2 x = 3$, then x is:

    a. 9

    b. 8

    c. 7

    d. 6

10. Solve the equation $\log_4 1/4 = x$.

    a. -1

    b. 0

    c. 1

    d. 2

Sequences

11. If $a_0 = 3$ and $a_n = -a_{n-1} + 3$, find a_3 of the sequence $\{a_n\}$.

    a. 0

    b. 1

    c. 2

    d. 3

12. If terms of the sequence $\{a_n\}$ are represented by $a_n = a_{n-1}/n$ and $a_1 = 1$, find a_4.

    a. 1/2

    b. 1/4

    c. 1/16

    d. 1/24

Answer Key

Geometry

1. B
We see that there is a square with side 2 cm and a rectangle adjacent to it, with one side 2 cm (common side with the square) and the other side 4 cm. The perimeter of a shape is found by summing up all sides surrounding the shape, not adding the ones inside the shape. Three 2 cm sides from the square, and two 4 cm sides and one 2 cm side from the rectangle contribute the perimeter.

So, the perimeter of the shape is: $2 + 2 + 2 + 4 + 2 + 4 = 16$ cm.

2. C
In the figure, we are given a large circle and a small circle inside it; with the diameter equal to the radius of the large one. The diameter of the small circle is 4 cm. This means that its radius is 2 cm. Since the diameter of the small circle is the radius of the large circle, the radius of the large circle is 4 cm. The area of a circle is calculated by: πr^2 where r is the radius.

Area of the small circle: $\pi(2)^2 = 4\pi$

Area of the large circle: $\pi(4)^2 = 16\pi$

The difference area is found by:

Area of the large circle - Area of the small circle = $16\pi - 4\pi = 12\pi$

3. B
We see that there are three squares forming a right triangle in the middle. Two of the squares have the areas 81 m^2 and 144 m^2. If we denote their sides a and b respectively:

$a^2 = 81$ and $b^2 = 144$. The length which is asked is the hypotenuse; a and b are the opposite and adjacent sides of the right angle. By using the Pythagorean Theorem, we can find the value of the asked side:

Pythagorean Theorem:
(Hypotenuse)^2 = (Perpendicular)^2 + (Base)^2
$h^2 = a^2 + b^2$

$a^2 = 81$, $b^2 = 144$
$h^2 = a^2 + b^2$
$h^2 = 81+144$
$h^2 = 225$
$h = 15$

Trigonometry

4. C
To understand this question better, draw a right triangle by writing the given data on it:

The side opposite to angle a is named by a.

cos a = length of the adjacent side / length of the hypotenuse

The length of the hypotenuse is found by the Pythagorean Theorem:

$a^2 + b^2 = c^2$ ... Here, c is the hypotenuse.

$8^2 + 6^2 = c^2$

$64 + 36 = c^2$

$100 = c^2$ → c = 10 So,

cos a = length of the adjacent side / length of the hypotenuse

cos a = b / c

cos a = 6 / 10 ... simplifying by 2;

cos a = 3 /5

5. D
When a figure is not given, in a right triangle, sides a

and b are the adjacent and opposite sides, and c is the hypotenuse. The angle and the side opposite to it are named in the same way (a and a).

To understand this question better, draw a right triangle by writing the given data on it:

The side opposite to angle a is named by a.

tan a = length of the opposite side / length of the adjacent side

tan a = a/b

tan a = 3/5

6. C

We know that sinx = cos(90° - x); sin30° = 1/2 and cos60° = sin30° = ½

So;

sin30° + cos60° = 1/2 + 1/2 = 1

Inequalities

7. C

To solve an inequality, we aim to leave x alone; without factors on one side, and the other numbers on the other side of the inequality sign:

-7x - 1 ≥ 13 … first, we add 1 to both sides:

-7x - 1 + 1 ≥ 13 + 1

-7x ≥ 14 … second, we divide both sides by 7:

-7x/7 ≥ 14/7

-x ≥ 2 … last, we multiply both sides by -1 to obtain a positive x. It is important not to forget that if we divide or multiply an inequality by a negative number, the inequality changes its direction:

$x \leq -2$ ... This is the solution. This means that x can be equal to -2 or a smaller value. So, $(-\infty, -2]$ **is the solution.**

8. D
$2x - 1 \geq x + 10$ ... first, we need to collect similar terms in the same side:

$2x - x - 1 \geq 10$

$x - 1 \geq 10$

$x \geq 10 + 1$

$x \geq 11$ ... this means that x can be 11 or a higher value; there is no upper limit for x, but lower limit is 11; including 11. This is shown as $[11, +\infty)$.

Logarithms

9. B
$\log_2 x = 3$ ... We aim to find x; so we need to have it alone in the equation. For this; first we need to eliminate the logarithm on the left side. In order to do this, we need to show 3 in the form of logarithm at base 2. We will use the following properties:

$\log_a a = 1$ ... (I)

$\log_a a^b = b \cdot \log_a a = b \cdot 1 = b$ ... (II)

Now, let us apply these rules to the question:

$\log_2 x = 3$

$\log_2 x = \log_2 2^3$ ... using property (II). So, since $2^3 = 8$;

$\log_2 x = \log_2 8$

Since 2 based logarithm is applied to both sides, x should be equal to 8.

$x = 8$

10. A -1

$\log_4 1/4 = x.$
$4x = 1/4$
$4x = 4-1$
$x = -1$

Sequences

11. A

We are given that,

$a_0 = 3$

$a_n = -a_{n-1} + 3$

Starting from the zeroth term, we can reach the third term:

$n = 1 \ldots a_1 = -a_0 + 3 = -3 + 3 = 0$

$n = 2 \ldots a_2 = -a_1 + 3 = 0 + 3 = 3$

$n = 3 \ldots a_3 = -a_2 + 3 = -3 + 3 = 0$

12. D

We are given that,

$a_1 = 1$

$a_n = a_{n-1}/n$

Starting from the first term, we can reach the fourth term:

$n = 2 \ldots a_2 = a_1/2 = 1/2$

$n = 3 \ldots a_3 = a_2/3 = (1/2)/3 = 1/6$

$n = 4 \ldots a_4 = a_3/4 = (1/6)/4 = 1/24$

Cartesian Plane, Coordinate Plane and Coordinate Grid

To locate dots and draw lines and curves, we use the coordinate plane. It also called Cartesian coordinate plane. It is a two-dimensional surface with a coordinate grid in it, which helps us to count the units. For the counting of those units, we use x-axis (horizontal scale) and y-axis (vertical scale).

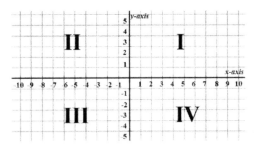

The whole system is called a coordinate system which is divided into 4 parts, called quadrants. The quadrant where all numbers are positive is the 1st quadrant (I), and if we go counterclockwise, we mark all 4 quadrants.

The location of a dot in the coordinate system is represented by coordinates. Coordinates are represented as a pair of numbers, where the 1st number is located on the x-axis and the 2nd number is located on the y-axis. So, if a dot A has coordinates a and b, then we write:

A=(a,b)   or   A(a,b)

The point where x-axis and y-axis intersect is called an origin. The origin is the point from which we measure the distance along the x and y axes.

In the Cartesian coordinate system we can calculate the distance between 2 given points. If we have dots with coordinates:
A=(a,b)
B=(c,d)

Then the distance d between A and B can be calculated by the following formula:

$$d = \sqrt{(c-a)^2 + (d-b)^2}$$

Cartesian coordinate system is used for the drawing of 2-dimentional shapes, and is also commonly used for functions.

Example:

Draw the function   y = (1 - x)/2

To draw a linear function, we need at least 2 points.
If we put that x=0 then value for y would be:

$$y = \frac{1-x}{2} = \frac{1-0}{2} = \frac{1}{2}$$

We found the 1st point, let's name it A, with following coordinates:

A = (0,1/2)

To find the 2nd point, we can put that x=1. In this case, the value for y would be:

$$y = \frac{1-x}{2} = \frac{1-1}{2} = \frac{0}{2} = 0$$

If we denote the 2nd point with B, then the coordinates for this point are:

B=(1,0)

Since we have 2 points necessary for the function, we find them in the coordinate system and we connect them with a line that represents the function,

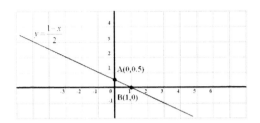

Perimeter Area and Volume

Perimeter and Area (2-dimentional shapes)

Perimeter of a shape determines the length around that shape, while the area includes the space inside the shape.

Rectangle:

$P = 2a + 2b$
$A = ab$

Square

$P = 4a$
$A = a^2$

Parallelogram

$P = 2a + 2b$
$A = ah_a = bh_b$

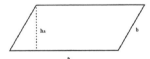

Rhombus

$P = 4a$
$A = ah = d_1 d_2 / 2$

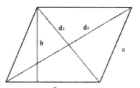

Triangle

$P = a + b + c$
$A = ah_a/2 = bh_b/2 = ch_c/2$

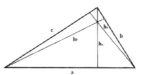

Equilateral Triangle

$P = 3a$
$A = (a^2\sqrt{3})/4$

Trapezoid

$P = a + b + c + d$
$A = ((a + b)/2)h$

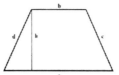

Circle

$P = 2r \prod$
$A = r^2 \prod$

Area and Volume (3-dimentional shapes)

To calculate the area of a 3-dimentional shape, we calculate the areas of all sides and then we add them all.

To find the volume of a 3-dimentional shape, we multiply the area of the base (B) and the height (H) of the 3-dimentional shape.

$$V = BH$$

In case of a pyramid and a cone, the volume would be divided by 3.

$$V = BH/3$$

Here are some of the 3-dimentional shapes with formulas for their area and volume:

Cuboids

$A = 2(ab + bc + ac)$
$V = abc$

Cube

$A = 6a^2$
$V = a^3$

Pyramid

$A = ab + ah_a + bh_b$

$V = abH/3$

Cylinder

$A = 2r^2 \prod + 2r\prod H$
$V = r^2\prod H$

Cone

$A = (r + s)r\prod$
$V = (r^2\prod H)/3$

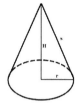

Pythagorean Geometry

If we have a right triangle ABC, where its sides (legs) are a and b and c is a hypotenuse (the side opposite the right angle), then we can establish a relationship between these sides using the following formula:

$c^2 = a^2 + b^2$

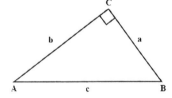

This formula is proven in the Pythagorean Theorem. There are many proofs of this theorem, but we'll look at just one geometrical proof:

If we draw squares on the right triangle's sides, then the area of the square on the hypotenuse is equal to the sum of the areas of the squares that are on other two sides of the triangle. Since the areas of these squares are a^2, b^2 and c^2, that is how we got the formula above.

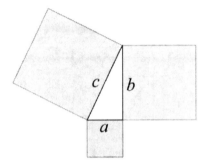

One of the famous right triangles is one with sides 3, 4 and 5. And we can see here that:

$3^2 + 4^2 = 5^2$
$9 + 16 = 25$
$25 = 25$

Example Problem:

The isosceles triangle ABC has a perimeter of 18 centimeters, and the difference between its base and legs is 3 centimeters. Find the height of this triangle.

We write the information we have about triangle ABC and we draw a picture of it for better understanding of the relation

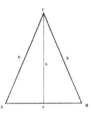

between its elements:

P=18 cm
a - b = 3 cm
h=?

We use the formula for the perimeter of the isosceles triangle, since that is what is given to us:

P=a+2b=18 cm

Notice that we have 2 equations with 2 variables, so we can solve it as a system of equations:

a + 2b = 18
a − b = 3 / a + 2b = 18
2a - 2b = 6 / a + 2b + 2a - 2b = 18 + 6
3a = 24
a = 24/3 = 8 cm

Now we go back to find b:
a - b = 3
8 - b = 3
b = 8 - 3
b = 5 cm

Using Pythagorean Theorem, we can find the height using a and b, because the height falls on the side at a right angle. Notice that height cuts side a exactly in half, and that's why we use in the formula a/2. Here, b is our hypotenuse, so we have:

$b^2 = (a/2)^2 + h^2$
$h^2 = b^2 - (a/2)^2$
$h^2 = 5^2 - (8/2)^2$
$h^2 = 5^2 - (8/2)^2$
$h^2 = 25 - 4^2$
$h^2 = 26 - 16$
$h^2 = 9$
$h = 3$ cm.

Quadrilaterals

Quadrilaterals are 2-dimentional geometrical shapes that have 4 sides and 4 angles. There are many types of quadrilaterals, depending on the length of its sides and if they are parallel and also depending on the size of its angles. All quadrilaterals have the following properties:

Sum of all interior angles is 360^0

Sum of all exterior angles is 360^0

A quadrilateral is a parallelogram is it fulfills at least one of the following conditions:

Angles on each side are supplementary
Opposite angles are equal
Opposite sides are equal
Diagonals intersect each other exactly in half

Here are some of the quadrilaterals:

Square

All sides are equal
All angles are right angles

Rectangle

2 pairs of equal sides
All angles are right angles

Parallelogram

2 pairs of equal sides
Opposite angles are equal

Rhombus

All sides are equal
Opposite angles are equal

Trapezoid

One pair of parallel sides

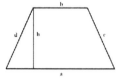

Example Problem
Find all angles of a parallelogram if one angle is greater than
the other one by 40^0.

First, we draw an image of a parallelogram:

We denote angles by α and β, Since this is a parallelogram,
the opposite angles are equal.

We are given that one angle is greater than the other one by
40^0, so we can write:

$β = α + 40^0$

We solve this problem in two ways:
1) The sum of all internal angles of every quadrilateral is
360^0. There are 2 α and 2 β. So we have:
$2α + 2β = 360^0$

Now, instead of β we write α + 40:
$2α + 2(α + 40^0) = 360^0$
$2α + 2α + 80^0 = 360^0$
$4α = 360^0 - 80^0$
$4α = 280^0$
$α = 280^0 / 4$
$α = 70^0$
Now we can find β from α:
$β = α + 40^0$
$β = 70^0 + 40^0$
$β = 110^0$

2) One of the conditions for parallelogram is "Angles on each side are supplementary" and we can use that to find these angles:

$\alpha + \beta = 180^0$

$\alpha + \alpha + 40^0 = 180^0$

$2\alpha = 180^0 - 40^0$

$2\alpha = 140^0$

$\alpha = 70^0$

Now we find β:

$\beta = \alpha + 40^0$

$\beta = 70^0 + 40^0$

$\beta = 110^0$

Trigonometry

If we are observing a right triangle, where a and b are its legs and c is its hypotenuse, we can use trigonometric functions to make a relationship between angles and sides of the right triangle.

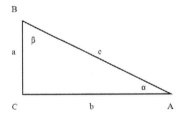

If the right angle of the right triangle ABC is at the point C, then the sine (sin) and the cosine (cos) of the angles α (at the point A) and β (at the point B) can be found like this:

$$sin\alpha = a/c \qquad sin\beta = b/c$$
$$cos\alpha = b/c \qquad cos\beta = a/c$$

Notice that $sin\alpha$ and $cos\beta$ are the equal, and same goes for $sin\beta$ and $cos\alpha$. So, to find sine of the angle, we divide the side that is opposite of that angle and the hypotenuse. To find cosine of the angle, we divide the side that makes that angle (adjacent side) by the hypotenuse.

There are 2 more important trigonometric functions, tangent and cotangent:

$$tg\alpha= sin\alpha/cos\alpha=a/b$$
$$ctg\alpha= cos\alpha/sin\alpha=b/a$$

For the functions sine and cosine, there is a table with values for some of the angles, which is to be memorized as it is very useful for solving various trigonometric problems. Here is that table:

	0^0	30^0	45^0	60^0	90^0
sinα	0	1/2	$\sqrt{2}/2$	$\sqrt{3}/2$	1
cosα	1	$\sqrt{3}/2$	$\sqrt{2}/2$	1/2	0

Let's see an example:

If a is 9 cm and c is 18 cm, find α.
We can use the sine for this problem:
$$sin\alpha=a/c=9/18=1/2$$
We can see from the table that if sinα is 1/2, then angle α is 30^0.

Besides degrees we can write angles using π, where π represents 180^0. For example, angle π/2 means a right angle of 90^0.

Solving inequalities

Basic linear inequalities have one of the following form:

$ax + b > 0$
$ax + b < 0$
$ax + b \geq 0$
$ax + b \leq 0$

where a and b are some real numbers. Our solution to any of these inequalities would be some interval. Let's see one simple example:

$2x - 10 > 16$
$2x > 16 + 10$
$2x > 26/2$
$x > 13$

So, the interval here is:

$(3, + \infty)$

If we have a case where –x is lesser or greater than some number, then we multiply the whole inequality by -1, where the sign of inequality also changes:

$-3x + 9 \leq 12$
$-3x \leq 12 - 9$
$-3x \leq 3$
$-x \leq 3/-1$
$x \leq -3$

So, the interval here is: $(3, + \infty)$ Notice the difference in the brackets. This is because this interval contains number 3.

Let's see a little more complex example:

$X/X + 1 > 0$

Whenever we have a fraction, we have to make a table:

		-1		0	
x	-		-		+
x+1	-		+		+
x/ X + 1	+		-		+

x is positive on the right of the 0, negative on the left of the 0. x+1 is positive on right of the -1, and negative on the left of the -1. If we multiply the signs, we get the signs for the function. We are interested in the positive sign (because we need it to be greater than 0), so the interval is:

$(-\infty, -1) \cup (0, +\infty)$

Logarithms

Logarithm is a function that has the form

$$\log_y x = a$$

It actually solves this equation: which number do we put as a degree on the variable y to get the variable x, that is:

$$y^a = x$$
y is called the base and a is the exponent.
For example, let's solve logarithm $\log_5 25 = a$.

$$5^a = 25$$
$$5^a = 5^2$$
$$a = 2$$

Here, we represent 25 using 5 and the second degree. a and 2 are both on the number 5, so they must be the same.

We can see from the way the logarithm works, that:

$$\log_a 1 = 0 \text{ and } \log_a a = 1$$

From $\log_a 1 = 0$ we have that $a^0 = 1$, which is true for any real number a.

From $\log_a a = 1$ we have that $a^1 = a$, which is true for any real number a.
If in the logarithm the base is 10, then instead of $\log_{10}$ we write l_g.

When we are solving some logarithm, any part can be unknown. In the first example, we had a case where the exponent was the unknown variable. Let's see another example, where both exponent and base are known:

$$l_g x = 2$$
$$10^2 = x$$
$$x = 100$$

Sequences

A sequence of numbers is a set of numbers, but here they are in order. For example, we can represent the set of natural numbers N as a sequence 1, 2, 3,... A sequence can be finite or infinite. In our case of the sequence of the natural numbers, we have an infinite sequence.

If we have a sequence of numbers a_1, a_2, a_3,... we denote that sequence by $\{a_n\}$. We can write, for example, the sequence of natural numbers like this:

$$a_n = a_{n-1} + 1 \text{ or } a_{n+1} = a_n + 1$$

From this formula, we can see that each number is greater than the previous number by one, which is true for the sequence of the natural numbers.

The first term (member) of the sequence is denoted by a_0. So, if we know the first term of the sequence and we know the formula that describes the sequence, we can find any term of that sequence. Even if we know some other member of the

sequence, we can find other members.
Let's solve 2 examples for both cases:

1) If $a_0 = 2$ and $a_n = a_{n-1} - 2$, find the 4th member of the sequence $\{a_n\}$.

Let's find 2nd and 3rd member, which we will use to find the 4th.

$$a_1 = a_0 - 2 = 2 - 2 = 0$$
$$a_2 = a_1 - 2 = 0 - 2 = -2$$
$$a_3 = a_2 - 2 = -2 - 2 = -4$$

So, our 4th member is number -4.

2) If $a_2 = 4$ and $a_n = 2a_{n-1}$, find the 1st member of the sequence $\{a_n\}$.

$$a_2 = 2a_1 \quad \rightarrow \quad 4 = 2a_1 \quad \rightarrow \quad a_1 = 2$$
$$a_1 = 2\,a_0 \quad \rightarrow \quad 2 = 2a_0 \quad \rightarrow \quad a_0 = 1$$

So, our first member is 1.

Sentence Skills

THIS SECTION CONTAINS A SELF-ASSESSMENT AND SENTENCE SKILLS TUTORIALS. The tutorials are designed to familiarize general principles and the self-assessment contains general questions similar to the sentence skills questions likely to be on the Accuplacer® exam, but are not intended to be identical to the exam questions. The tutorials are not designed to be a complete course, and it is assumed that students have some familiarity with sentence skills. If you do not understand parts of the tutorial, or find the tutorial difficult, it is recommended that you seek out additional instruction.

Tour of the Accuplacer® Sentence skills Content

The Accuplacer® sentence skills section has 20 questions. Below is a list of the likely sentence skills topics likely to appear on the Accuplacer®. Make sure that you understand these topics at the very minimum.

- English grammar

- English usage

- Punctuation

- Subject - verb agreement

- Sentence structure

The questions in the self-assessment are not the same as you will find on the Accuplacer® - that would be too easy! And nobody knows what the questions will be and they change all the time. Mostly, the changes consist of substituting new questions for old, but the changes also can be new question formats or styles, changes to the number of questions in each section, changes to the time limits for each section, and combining sections. So, while the format and exact wording of the questions may differ slightly, and changes from year to year, if you can answer the questions below, you will have no problem with the sentence skills section of the Accuplacer®.

Sentence skills Self-Assessment

The purpose of the self-assessment is:

- Identify your strengths and weaknesses.

- Develop your personalized study plan (above)

- Get accustomed to the Accuplacer® format

- Extra practice – the self-assessments are almost a full 3rd practice test!

- Provide a baseline score for preparing your study schedule.

Since this is a Self-assessment, and depending on how confident you are with sentence skills, timing yourself is optional. The Accuplacer® has 20 questions. This self-assessment has 20 questions, so allow about 20 minutes to complete.

Once complete, use the table below to assess your understanding of the content, and prepare your study schedule described in chapter 1.

80% - 100%	Excellent – you have mastered the content
60 – 79%	Good. You have a working knowledge. Even though you can just pass this section, you may want to review the tutorials and do some extra practice to see if you can improve your mark.
40% - 59%	Below Average. You do not understand the sentence skills content. Review the tutorials , and retake this quiz again in a few days, before proceeding to the practice test questions.
Less than 40%	Poor. You have a very limited understanding of the sentence skills content. Please review the tutorials , and retake this quiz again in a few days, before proceeding to the practice test questions.

Sentence Skills Answer Sheet

1. (A) (B) (C) (D)   11. (A) (B) (C) (D)

2. (A) (B) (C) (D)   12. (A) (B) (C) (D)

3. (A) (B) (C) (D)   13. (A) (B) (C) (D)

4. (A) (B) (C) (D)   14. (A) (B) (C) (D)

5. (A) (B) (C) (D)   15. (A) (B) (C) (D)

6. (A) (B) (C) (D)   16. (A) (B) (C) (D)

7. (A) (B) (C) (D)   17. (A) (B) (C) (D)

8. (A) (B) (C) (D)   18. (A) (B) (C) (D)

9. (A) (B) (C) (D)   19. (A) (B) (C) (D)

10. (A) (B) (C) (D)   20. (A) (B) (C) (D)

1. The older children <u>have already eat</u> their dinner, but the baby <u>has not yet ate anything</u>.

a. The older children have already eat their dinner, but the baby has not yet eaten anything.

b. The older children have already eaten their dinner, but the baby has not yet ate anything.

c. The older children have already eaten their dinner, but the baby has not eaten anything yet.

d. No change is necessary.

2. Its important for you to know <u>it's</u> official name; <u>it's</u> called the Confederate Museum.

a. Its important for you to know its official name; its called the Confederate Museum.

b. It's important for you to know it's official name; it's called the Confederate Museum.

c. It's important for you to know its official name; it's called the Confederate Museum.

d. No change is necessary.

3. He would have postponed the camping trip, if he <u>would have known</u> about the forecast.

a. No change is necessary.

b. If he would have known about the forecast, he would have postponed the camping trip.

c. If he have known about the forecast, he would have postponed the camping trip.

d. If he had known about the forecast, he would have postponed the camping trip.

4. He <u>don't have any</u> money to buy clothes and neither do I.

    a. He doesn't have any money to buy clothes and neither do I.

    b. He doesn't have any money to buy clothes and neither does I.

    c. He don't have any money to buy clothes and neither does I.

    d. No change is necessary.

5. Because it really doesn't matter, I <u>doesn't care</u> if I go there.

    a. Because it really don't matter, I don't care if I go there.

    b. Because it really doesn't matter, I don't care if I go there.

    c. Because it really don't matter, I don't care if I go there.

    d. No change is necessary

6. The mother <u>would not of</u> punished her daughter if she could of avoided it.

    a. The mother would not of punished her daughter if she could have avoided it.

    b. The mother would not have punished her daughter if she could of avoided it.

    c. No changes are necessary.

    d. The mother would not have punished her daughter if she could have avoided it.

7. There was scarcely <u>no food</u> in the pantry, because <u>not nobody</u> ate at home.

    a. There was scarcely no food in the pantry, because nobody ate at home.

    b. There was scarcely any food in the pantry, because nobody ate at home.

    c. There was scarcely any food in the pantry, because not nobody ate at home.

    d. No changes are necessary.

8. Michael <u>has lived</u> in that house for forty years, while I <u>have owned</u> this one for only six weeks.

    a. Michael has lived in that house for forty years, while I has owned this one for only six weeks.

    b. Michael have lived in that house for forty years, while I have owned this one for only six weeks.

    c. Michael have lived in that house for forty years, while I has owned this one for only six weeks.

    d. No change is necessary.

9. Lee pronounced <u>its</u> name incorrectly; <u>it's</u> an impatiens, not an impatience.

    a. Lee pronounced it's name incorrectly; it's an impatiens, not an impatience.

    b. Lee pronounced its name incorrectly; its an impatiens, not an impatience.

    c. Lee pronounced it's name incorrectly; its an impatiens, not an impatience.

    d. No change is necessary.

10. After the car was fixed it <u>ran good</u> again.

    a. No change is necessary.

    b. After the car was fixed it ran well again.

    c. After the car was fixed it would have run well again.

    d. After the car was fixed it ran more well again.

11. Reading off a computer screen can hurt the eyes, but it is often more convenient.

Rewrite, beginning with

Although often more convenient,

The next words will be

    a. it can hurt to

    b. but reading off a computer screen can

    c. reading off a computer screen can

    d. you can hurt your eyes by

12. Leafcutter ants do not eat the leaves, but use them to grow fungus in the colony.

Rewrite, beginning with

Instead of eating the leaves,

The next words will be

    a. leafcutter ants use them to

    b. fungus use them to

    c. fungus in the colony grows

    d. growing fungus in the colony

13. Lydia will not finish the race unless she sleeps well the night before.

Rewrite, beginning with

If she does not sleep well the night before,

The next words will be

    a. unless Lydia will not
    b. Lydia will not
    c. finishing the race
    d. Lydia will finish

14. Before playing a guitar solo, he sang the chorus.

Rewrite, beginning with

After singing the chorus,

The next words will be

    a. he played
    b. a guitar solo
    c. and then he played
    d. and then a guitar solo

15. Samuel saw no ships as he scanned the horizon.

Rewrite, beginning with

Scanning the horizon,

The next words will be

    a. no ships could be seen
    b. seeing no ships
    c. and Samuel saw
    d. Samuel saw no ships

16. Hippos spend most of the day in water, since they need to keep cool.

Rewrite, beginning with

Needing to keep cool,

The next words will be

    a. most of the day

    b. hippos spend

    c. in water hippos spend

    d. it is most of the day

17. Even though sharks prefer the taste of fish, they may bite humans out of curiosity.

Rewrite, beginning with

Sharks may bite humans out of curiosity,

The next words will be

    a. and they prefer

    b. but they prefer

    c. preferring the taste of

    d. and the taste of

18. Much larger than tornadoes, hurricanes usually cause more damage.

Rewrite, beginning with

Since they are much smaller than hurricanes,

The next words will be

    a. causing less damage

    b. less damage is

    c. tornadoes usually cause more

    d. tornadoes usually cause less

19. Despite its fear of humans, sometimes the black bear will venture into town in search of food.

Rewrite, beginning with

The black bear fears humans,

The next words will be

      a. but will sometimes venture into

      b. venturing into

      c. and will sometimes venture into

      d. despite to venture into

20. Had he studied last night, Kevin would have aced his exam.

Rewrite, beginning with

Kevin would have aced his exam

The next words will be

      a. having studied

      b. as he had studied

      c. although he had studied

      d. if he had studied

Answer Key

1. C
Present perfect. You cannot use the Present Perfect with specific time expressions such as: yesterday, one year ago, last week, when I was a child, at that moment, that day, one day, etc. The Present Perfect is used with unspecific expressions such as: ever, never, once, many times, several times, before, so far, already, yet, etc.

2. C
Its vs. It's. It's is a contraction for it is or it has. Its is a possessive pronoun meaning, more or less, of it or belonging to it.

3. D
The third conditional is used for talking about an unreal situation (that did not happen) in the past. For example, "If I had studied harder, [if clause] I would have passed the exam [main clause]. Which is the same as, "I failed the exam, because I didn't study hard enough."

4. A
Disagreeing with a negative statement uses "neither."

5. C
Doesn't, does not, or does is used with the third person singular--words like he, she, and it. Don't, do not, or do is used for other subjects.

6. D
The third conditional is used for talking about an unreal situation (that did not happen) in the past. For example, "If I had studied harder, [if clause] I would have passed the exam [main clause]. Which is the same as, "I failed the exam, because I didn't study hard enough."

7. B
Double negative sentence. In double negative sentences, one of the negatives is replaced with "any."

8. D
Present perfect. You cannot use the Present Perfect with specific time expressions such as: yesterday, one year ago, last week, when I was a child, at that moment, that day, one day, etc. The Present Perfect is used with unspecific expressions such as: ever, never, once, many times, several times, before, so far, already, yet, etc.

9. D
Its vs. It's. It's is a contraction for it is or it has. Its is a possessive pronoun meaning, more or less, of it or belonging to it.

10. B
Present tense, "ran well" is correct. "Ran good" is never correct.

11. C
"Convenient" must be directly followed by "reading," which it modifies.

12. A
"Instead of" has replaced "but" in the opposing clause, and the action of "eating" must be attributed to "leafcutter ants," not to "fungus."

13. B
"If...not" has replaced "unless" in the subordinate clause, and the main clause must begin with "Lydia," the subject of the sentence and antecedent of "she."

14. A
The order is: chorus, and then solo. The second clause must be a main clause beginning with "he."

15. D
"Scanning" must modify "Samuel," which is the subject of the main clause.

16. B
"Needing" must modify and therefore be as close as possible to "hippos," the subject of the main clause.

17. B
"But" must replace "even though" as the opposing conjunction.

18. D
"They" must refer to "tornadoes" in the main clause. The damage done by tornadoes is less.

19. A
"But" replaces "despite" as the opposing conjunction; and only "will venture" exhibits correct grammatical structure.

20. D
"If he had" is the only option that retains the meaning of "had he."

Common English Usage Mistakes - A Quick Review

Like some parts of English grammar, usage is definitely going to be on the exam and there isn't any tricky strategies or shortcuts to help you get through this section.
Here is a quick review of common usage mistakes.

1. May and Might

'May' can act as a principal verb, which can express permission or possibility.

Examples:

Lets wait, the meeting may have started.
May I begin now?

'May' can act as an auxiliary verb, which an expresses a purpose or wish

Examples:

May you find favour in the sight of your employer.

May your wishes come true.
People go to school so that they may be educated.

The past tense of may is might.

Examples:

I asked if I might begin

'Might' can be used to signify a weak or slim possibility or polite suggestion.

Examples:

You might find him in his office, but I doubt it.
You might offer to help if you want to.

2. Lie and Lay

The verb lay should always take an object. The three forms of the verb lay are: laid, lay and laid.

The verb lie (recline) should not take any object. The three forms of the verb lie are: lay, lie and lain.

Examples:

Lay on the bed.
The tables were laid by the students.
Let the little kid lie.
The patient lay on the table.

The dog has lain there for 30 minutes.

Note: The verb lie can also mean "to tell a falsehood." This verb can appear in three forms: lied, lie, and lied. This is different from the verb lie (recline) mentioned above.

Examples:

The accused is fond of telling lies.
Did she lie?

3. Would and should

The past tense of shall is 'should', and so "should" generally follows the same principles as "shall."

The past tense of will is "would," and so "would" generally follows the same principles as "will."

The two verbs 'would and should' can be correctly used interchangeably to signify obligation. The two verbs also have some unique uses too. Should is used in three persons to signify obligation.

Examples:

I should go after work.
People should do exercises everyday.
You should be generous.

"Would" is specially used in any of the three persons, to signify willingness, determination and habitual action.
Examples:

They would go for a test run every Saturday.
They would not ignore their duties.
She would try to be punctual.

4. Principle and Auxiliary Verbs

Two principal verbs can be used along with one auxiliary verb as long as the auxiliary verb form suits the two principal verbs.

Examples:

A number of people have been employed and some promoted.

A new tree has been planted and the old has been cut down.

Again note the difference in the verb form.

5. Can and Could

A. Can is used to express capacity or ability.

Examples:

I can complete the assignment today
He can meet up with his target.

B. Can is also used to express permission.

Examples:

Yes, you can begin

In the sentence below, "can" was used to mean the same thing as "may." However, the difference is that the word "can" is used for negative or interrogative sentences, while "may" is used in affirmative sentences to express possibility.

Examples:

They may be correct.   Positive sentence - use may.
Can this statement be correct? A question using "can."
It cannot be correct. Negative sentence using "can."

The past tense of can is could. It can serve as a principal verb when it is used to express its own meaning.

Examples:

In spite of the difficulty of the test, he could still perform well.
"Could" here is used to express ability.

6. Ought

The verb ought should normally be followed by the word to.

Examples:

I *ought to* close shop now.

The verb 'ought' can be used to express:

A. Desirability

You ought to wash your hands before eating.   It is desirable to wash your hands.

B. Probability

She ought to be on her way back by now.   She is probably on her way.

C. Moral obligation or duty

The government ought to protect the oppressed.   It is the government's duty to protect the oppressed.

7. Raise and Rise

Rise
The verb rise means to go up, or to ascend.
The verb rise can appear in three forms, rose, rise, and risen. The verb should not take an object.

Examples:

The bird rose very slowly.
The trees rise above the house.
My aunt has risen in her career.

Raise
The verb raise means to increase, to lift up.
The verb raise can appear in three forms, raised, raise and raised.

Examples:

He raised his hand.
The workers requested a raise.
Do not raise that subject.

8. Past Tense and Past Participle

Pay attention to the proper usage of these verbs: sing, show, ring, awake, fly, flow, begin, hang and sink.

Mistakes usually occur when using the past participle and past tense of these verbs as they are often mixed up.

Each of these verbs can appear in three forms:

Sing, Sang, Sung.
Show, Showed, Showed/Shown.
Ring, Rang, Rung.
Awake, awoke, awaken
Fly, Flew, Flown.
Flow, Flowed, Flowed.
Begin, Began, Begun.
Hang, Hanged, Hanged (a criminal)
Hang, Hung, Hung (a picture)
Sink, Sank, Sunk.

Examples:

The stranger rang the door bell. (simple past tense)
I have rung the door bell already. (past participle - an action completed in the past)

The stone sank in the river. (simple past tense)
The stone had already sunk. (past participle - an action completed in the past)

The meeting began at 4:00.
The meeting has begun.

9. Shall and Will

When speaking informally, the two can be used interchangeably. In formal writing, they must be used correctly.

"Will" is used in the second or third person, while "shall" is used in the first person. Both verbs are used to express a time or even in the future.

Examples:

I shall, We shall (First Person)
You will (Second Person)
They will (Third Person)

This principle however reverses when the verbs are to
be used to express threats, determination, command,
willingness, promise or compulsion. In these instances, will
is now used in first person and shall in the second and third
person.

Examples:

I will be there next week, no matter what.
This is a promise, so the first person "I" takes "will."

You shall ensure that the work is completed.
This is a command, so the second person "you" takes "shall."

I will try to make payments as promised.
This is a promise, so the first person "I" takes "will."

They shall have arrived by the end of the day.
This is a determination, so the third person "they" takes
shall.

Note
A. The two verbs, shall and will should not occur twice in the
same sentence when the same future is being referred to

Example:

I shall arrive early if my driver is here on time.

B. Will should not be used in the first person when
questions are being asked

Examples:

Shall I go ?
Shall we go?

Subject Verb Agreement

Verbs in any sentence must agree with the subject of the
sentence both in person and number. Problems usually
occur when the verb doesn't correspond with the right
subject or the verb fails to match the noun close to it.

Unfortunately, there is no easy way around these principals
- no tricky strategy or easy rule.   You just have to memorize
them.

Here is a quick review:

The verb to be, present (past)

Person	Singular	Plural
First	I am (was)	we are (were)
Second	you are (were)	you are (were)
Third	he, she, it is (was)	they are (were)

The verb to have, present (past)

Person	Singular	Plural
First	I have (had)	we have (had)
Second	you have (had)	you have (had)
Third	he, she, it has (had)	they have (had)

Regular verbs, e.g. to walk, present (past)

Person	Singular	Plural
First	I walk (walked)	we walk (walked)
Second	you walk (walked)	you walk (walked)
Third	he, she, it walks (walked)	they work (walked)

1. Every and Each

When nouns are qualified by "every" or "each," they take a singular verb even if they are joined by 'and'

Examples:

Each mother and daughter *was* a given separate test.
Every teacher and student *was* properly welcomed.

2. Plural Nouns

Nouns like measles, tongs, trousers, riches, scissors etc. are all plural.

Examples:

The trousers *are* dirty.
My scissors *have* gone missing.
The tongs *are* on the table.

3. With and As Well

Two subjects linked by "with" or "as well" should have a verb that matches the first subject.

Examples:

The pencil, with the papers and equipment, *is* on the desk.
David as well as Louis is coming.

4. Plural Nouns

The following nouns take a singular verb:

> politics, mathematics, innings, news, advice,
> summons, furniture, information, poetry, machinery,
> vacation, scenery

Examples:

The machinery *is* difficult to assemble
The furniture *has* been delivered
The scenery *was* beautiful

5. Single Entities

A proper noun in plural form that refers to a single entity requires a singular verb. This is a complicated way of saying; some things appear to be plural, but are really singular, or some nouns refer to a collection of things but the collection is really singular.

Examples:

The United Nations Organization *is* the decision maker in the matter.

Here the "United Nations Organization" is really only one "thing" or noun, but is made up of many "nations."

The book, "The Seven Virgins" *was* not available in the library.

Here there is only one book, although the title of the book is plural.

6. Specific Amounts are always singular

A plural noun that refers to a specific amount or quantity that is considered as a whole (dozen, hundred, score etc) requires a singular verb.

Examples:

60 minutes *is* quite a long time.
Here "60 minutes" is considered a whole, and therefore one item (singular noun).

The first million is the most difficult.

7. Either, Neither and Each are always singular

The verb is always singular when used with: either, each, neither, every one and many.

Examples:

Either of the boys *is* lying.
Each of the employees *has* been well compensated
Many a police officer *has* been found to be courageous
Every one of the teachers *is* responsible

8. Linking with Either, Or, and Neither match the second subject

Two subjects linked by "either," "or,""nor" or "neither" should have a verb that matches the second subject.

Examples:

Neither David nor Paul *will* be coming.
Either Mary or Tina *is* paying.

Note
If one of the subjects linked by "either," "or,""nor" or "neither" is in plural form, then the verb should also be in plural, and the verb should be close to the plural subject.

Examples:
Neither the mother *nor* her kids *have* eaten.
Either Mary *or* her *friends are* paying.

9. Collective Nouns are Plural

Some collective nouns such as poultry, gentry, cattle, vermin etc. are considered plural and require a plural verb.

Examples:

The *poultry are* sick.
The *cattle are* well fed.

Note
Collective nouns involving people can work with both plural and singular verbs.

Examples:

Nigerians are known to be hard working
Europeans live in Africa

10. Nouns that are Singular and Plural

Nouns like deer, sheep, swine, salmon etc. can be singular or plural and require the same verb form.

Examples:

The swine is feeding. (singular)
The swine are feeding. (plural)

The salmon is on the table. (singular)
The salmon are running upstream. (plural)

11. Collective Nouns are Singular

Collective nouns such as Army, Jury, Assembly, Committee, Team etc should carry a singular verb when they subscribe to one idea. If the ideas or views are more than one, then the verb used should be plural.

Examples:

The committee is in agreement in their decision.

The committee were in disagreement in their decision.
The jury has agreed on a verdict.
The jury were unable to agree on a verdict.

12. Subjects links by "and" are plural.

Two subjects linked by "and" always require a plural verb

Examples:

David and John are students.

Note
If the subjects linked by "and" are used as one phrase, or constitute one idea, then the verb must be singular

The color of his socks and shoe is black.
Here "socks and shoe" are two nouns, however the subject is "color" which is singular.

How to Write an Essay

Writing an essay can be a difficult process, especially if you are under time constraints such as during an exam. Here are three simple steps to help you to write a solid, well thought out essay:

1. **Brainstorm** potential themes and general ideas for your essay.

2. **Outline** your essay step by step, including subheadings for ease of understanding.

3. **Write** your essay carefully being aware of proper grammar and sentence structure.

Brainstorming

You should first spend some time thinking about the general subject of the essay. If the essay is asking a question, you must make sure to answer this fully in your essay. You may find it helpful to highlight key words in your assignment or use a simple spider diagram to jot down key ideas.

Example

Read the following information and complete the following assignment:

Joseph Conrad is a Polish author who lived in England for most of his life and wrote a prolific amount of English literature. Much of his work was completed during the height of the British Empire's colonial imperialism.

Assignment: What impact has Joseph Conrad had on modern society? Present your point of view on the matter and support it with evidence. Your evidence may include reasoning, logic, examples from readings, your own experience, and observations.

Joseph Conrad

Background? sailor, adventure, Polish immigrant, Youth, Nostromo, Heart of Darkness
Themes in his works? ivory, silver trading, colonialism, corruption, greed
Thoughts? descent into madness, nature of evil

Outlining (or planning)

An outline or plan is critical to organize your thoughts and ideas fully and logically. There are many ways to do this; the easiest is to write down the following headings:

1. Title
2. Introduction
3. Body
4. Conclusion

You should then jot down key ideas and themes that fit logically under the appropriate heading. This plan is now the backbone of your essay.

Tip: Even if you are not required to produce an outline or plan for the assignment, you should always leave it with your essay in the exam booklet or the back of the assignment paper. Simply draw a line across it and write 'plan' or 'outline'. This demonstrates to the reader the approach you use in formulating and finally writing your essay.

Writing the essay

Your introduction is what will help the reader to decide whether they want to read the rest of your essay. The introduction also introduces the subject matter and allows you to provide a general background to the reader. The first sentence is very important and you should avoid starting the essay with openers such as 'I will be comparing...'

Example

> Born as Józef Teodor Konrad Korzeniowski
> on December 3rd, 1857, Joseph Conrad led
> an adventurous life. As a Polish immigrant,
> Conrad never quite fit into England where
> he spent most of his adult life. As a younger
> man, Conrad made a living off sailing voyages.
> These swashbuckling experiences soon
> had him writing tales of the high seas such
> as one of his first works, Youth. While his
> early, adventurous work was of high quality,
> Conrad is best remembered for shedding
> light on the exploitative side of colonialism.
> Age and experience led him to start writing
> about (and challenging) the darker side of the
> imperial way of thinking. Conrad's work has
> forever soured words such as colonialism and
> imperialism.

In the main part, or body of your essay, you should always
be yourself and be original.

- Avoid using clichés.
- Be aware of your tone.
- Consider the language that you use. Avoid jargon
  and slang. Use clear prose and imagery.
- Your writing should always flow; remember to use
  transitions, especially between paragraphs. Read
  aloud in your head to make sure a paragraph sounds
  right.
- Always try to use a new paragraph for new ideas.

Example

> *Conrad's written fiction focused on themes*
> *such as greed and power. He portrayed these*
> *two concepts as purveyors of evil. Greed and*
> *power may take on different guises, but the*
> *end result would always be the same.*
>
> *Perhaps his most famous piece, The Heart of*
> *Darkness, is about the descent of an English*

ivory trader, Mr. Kurtz, into madness. We are taken up a river resembling the Congo by a narrator, Marlow, who is sent to retrieve Mr. Kurtz. Marlow eventually finds that Kurtz has been diluted by power and greed, the two things that spurred on colonialism in Africa. Kurtz has taken charge of a large tribe of natives (that he brutalizes) and has been hoarding ivory for himself.

Much of Conrad's later work was cut from the same vein as The Heart of Darkness. His crowning achievement is considered Nostromo where he takes an idealistic hero and corrupts him with colonial greed. Only this time the greed is for silver, not ivory.

Conrad's work resonates with readers partly because it was semi-autobiographical. Where his experience sailing the high seas helped bring his adventure stories to light, likewise did his experience witnessing atrocities in Africa reverberate through his writing.

The conclusion is your last chance to impress your reader and brings your entire essay to a logical close. You may want to link your conclusion back to your introduction or provide some closing statements. Do not panic if you cannot close your essay off completely. Few subjects offer closure.

Your conclusion should always be consistent with the rest of the essay and you should never introduce a new idea in your conclusion. It is also important to remember that a weak conclusion can diminish the impact of a good essay.

Example

In sum, Joseph Conrad's life experiences and masterful writing left a lasting impact on the image of progress and what it meant to "move forward." He brought to light the cost in human lives that was required for Europe to continue mining natural resources from foreign lands. Joseph Conrad had a permanent impact on imperial culture, and colonial brutality has been on the decline ever since his work was published.

Presentation

Poor grammar and punctuation can ruin an otherwise good essay. You should always follow any requirements about the presentation of your essay, such as word count. You should also make sure that your writing is legible. Always allow time for one final read-through before submission.

Tip: If you are able to, write with double spacing. If you make a mistake, you can cross it out and write the correction on the blank line above.

Some final points to think about for writing a solid, well thought out essay:

- A good essay will contain a strong focus.

- There is no set essay structure but you can use sub-headings for better readability.

- Avoid particularly sensitive or controversial material. If you must write about something controversial, always make sure to include counter arguments.

- Your essay may have little to do with the subject itself; it is about what you make of the subject.

- Your essay can include examples from your readings, experience, studies or observations.

- Spend time doing practice essays and looking at sample essays beforehand.

Another Example

Lets look at another example using the three steps required to write a good essay:

1. **Brainstorming**

2. **Outlining**

3. **Writing**

Using a second essay, we can now explore these three steps in further detail.

Brainstorming

Example

> *Think about the information that follows and the assignment below.*
>
> *People often quote the last two lines of Robert Frost's "The Road not Taken" as being metaphorical for success. The line's read "I took the one less travelled by, / And that has made all the difference" (19, 20).*
>
> *Assignment: Analyze and interpret this poem. Consider the poem's place in Modernist culture and Robert Frost's personal experiences. Read in between the lines and identify the more complex aspects/themes of this poem. Outline and complete an essay that challenges the point of view presented above, that the poem is synonymous with success. Provide evidence backed up by logic, experience, research, and/ or examples from the poem.*

The assignment and key words that appear in the brief above are being highlighted. This confirms that the essay is not asking a specific question, but rather, it is asking for discussion of the subject matter and phrases.

This is the time to take a few moments to jot down initial thoughts about the assignment. Do not worry too much about proper grammar at this point, just get all your thoughts down on paper:

"The Road Not Taken" by Robert Frost

> **Background?** Modernist poetry
> **Themes?** Life decisions, regret, fate, the unknown future
> **Thoughts?** The diverging roads are symbolic, the sigh at end signifies regret, life has many twists and turns, you can end up in a drastically different situation later after a simple decision now

Outlining (or Planning)

Outlining or planning is the next important stage in the process and you should always spend a few minutes writing a plan. This plan is just as important as the essay itself. You can also note how much **time** you may want to spend on a particular section. Make sure to assign headings to each main section of the essay and include important questions/themes you want to address.

Example

1. Title

2. Essay introduction
Identify and discuss the underlying theme/s in Robert Frost's "The Road Not Taken"
What was Frost's background and its applicability to understanding this poem?

3. Essay body
Quick summary of the poem
Discuss key themes and other concepts
Discuss how these things relate to Modernism

4. Essay conclusion
Rephrase the themes of Robert Frost's poem

and their place in modernist doctrine

This plan is now the outline for the essay.

Writing the Essay

The introduction is important, as it needs to introduce the reader to the essay in a way that will encourage them to continue reading. A good introduction will introduce the subject matter to a reader and point out relevant information that may be helpful to know when reading the rest of the essay.

Example

> Identify and discuss the underlying theme/s in Robert Frost's "The Road Not Taken"
>
> *Robert Frost wrote during the artistic movement after World War I known as Modernism. One purpose of modernism was to remake things in a new light, to analyze and change symptoms of societies that had plunged the European world into a grisly war. Frost's poem, "The Road Not Taken," carries with it a burden of regret that was a staple of Modernist art.*

This introduction opens with what explaining about the time period of Robert Frost and real life influences to the theme of his poem, "The Road Not Taken." It contains some powerful language that will encourage the reader to continue reading and gives a solid base in understanding the remainder of the essay.

The main part or **body of the essay** is also very important:

Example

> *"The Road Not Taken" was almost assuredly influenced by Robert Frost's personal life. He was very familiar with facing difficult decisions. Frost had to make the decision to send both his sister and daughter to mental institutions. His son Carol committed suicide at the age of 38. The list of loss Frost experienced in*

his life goes on, but it suffices to say he was familiar with questioning the past.

With no other hints of the narrator's identity, it is best to assume that he is a man similar to Frost himself. The poem itself is about a nameless narrator reflecting on when he travelled through the autumn woods one day. He had come across a split in the road and expresses regret that he could not travel both. Each road is described as looking similar and as having equal wear but it is also mentioned one was grassier. The roads were unknown to the narrator, and shared equal possibilities in how well they may or may not be around their bends. He tells his listener with a sigh that he had made his decision and had taken "the road less travelled by" (19). Even though he had little idea which road would be better in the long run, the one he chose proved difficult.

This poem is a collection of all the insecurities and possibilities that come with even the simplest decisions. We experience the sorrow expressed by the narrator in the opening lines with every decision we make. For all the choices you make in life, there is a counterweight of choices you have not made. In a way, we are all missing half of our lives' possibilities. This realization causes a mixture of regret and nostalgia, but also stokes in us the keen awareness that missed opportunities are inevitable and regretting them is a waste of energy. We often find ourselves stuck, as the narrator is, between questioning the decisions we've made and knowing that this natural process isn't exactly productive.

Unsolvable regret and nostalgia are things that the Modernists fought with on a regular basis. They often experimented in taking happenings of the past and reinventing them to fit a new future.

The body of the essay opens with providing a brief overview of Robert Frost's personal life and his life's relevance to the over arching theme of dealing with difficult decisions in the poem, "The Road Not Taken."

A new paragraph starts where appropriate and at the end of the discussion of Robert Frost's life, a **transition** moves the reader back to the start of the book (closing off this section). This also helps to move the reader towards the next discussion point.

The tone of this essay is formal, mainly because of the seriousness of the subject – regret and nostalgia plays a major role in people's lives all around the world.

For the conclusion, there will be a summary of the main discussion. While it is ideal for you to impress the reader with your writing, more importantly you need to make sure you cover all your bases and address the assignment appropriately with a closing statement about any important points you discussed in the body of your essay.

Example

> *In conclusion, Robert Frost's poem "The Road Not Taken" deals with themes of fate, regret, sorrow, and the many possibilities our decisions hold. Consider how easy it would be to upturn your life today if you made a few decisions you normally wouldn't. Frost's poem forces us to consider the twists and turns our lives take. Perhaps with a sigh, we could all think about the choices that for us have made all the difference.*

This conclusion is consistent with the rest of the essay in terms of style. There are no new ideas introduced and it has referred to the main points in the assignment title.

Finally, a full read-through is necessary before submission. It only takes a couple of minutes to read through and pick up any errors. Remember to double space to leave room for any corrections to be made. You can also leave spacing at the end of each paragraph in case you should need to add an additional sentence or two.

Common Essay Mistakes - Example 1

Whether the topic is love or action, reality television shows damage society. Viewers witness the personal struggles of strangers and they experience an outpouring of emotions in the name of entertainment. This can be dangerous on many levels. Viewers become numb to real emotions and values. Run the risk of not interpreting a dangerous situation correctly. 1 The reality show participant is also at risk because they are completely exposed. 2 The damage to both viewers and participants leads to the destruction of our healthy societal values.

Romance reality shows are dangerous to the participants and contribute to the emotional problems witnessed in society today as we set up a system built on equality and respect, shows like "The Bachelor" tear it down. 3 In front of millions of viewers every week, young women compete for a man. Twenty-five women claim to be in love with a man they just met. The man is reduced to an object they compete for. There are tears, fights, and manipulation aimed at winning the prize. 4 Imagine a young woman's reality when she returns home and faces the scrutiny of viewers who watched her unravel on television every Monday night. These women objectify themselves and have learned 5 that relationships are a combination of hysteria and competition. This does not give hope to a society based on family values and equality.

6 While incorporating the same manipulations and breakdown of relationships offered on "The Bachelor," shows like "Survivor" add another level of danger. Not only are they building a society based on lying to each other, they are competing in physical challenges that become dangerous. In the name of entertainment, these challenges become increasingly physical and are usually held in a hostile environment. The viewer's ability to determine the safety of an activity is messed up. 7 To entertain and preserve their pride, participants continue in competitions regardless of the danger level. For example, 8 participants on "Survivor" have sustained serious injuries as heart attack and burns.

Societal rules are based on the safety of its citizens, not on hurting yourself for entertainment.

Reality shows of all kinds are dangerous to participants. They damage society. 9

1. Correct sentence fragments. Who/what runs the risk? Add a subject or combine sentences. Try: "Viewers become numb to real emotions and run the risk of not interpreting a dangerous situation correctly."

2. Correct redundant phrases. Try: "The reality show participant is also at risk because they are exposed."

3. Correct run-on sentences. Decide which thoughts should be separated. Try: "Romance reality shows are dangerous to participants and contribute to the emotional problems of society today. As we support a system built on equality and respect, shows like "The Bachelor" tear it down."

4. Vary sentence structure and length. Try: "Twenty-five women claim to be in love with a man who is reduced to being the object of competition. There are tears, fights, and manipulation aimed at winning the prize."

5. Use active voice. Try: These women objectify themselves and learned that relationships are a combination of hysteria and competition.

6. Use transitions to tie paragraphs together. Try: Start the paragraph with, "Action oriented reality shows are equally as dangerous to the participants."

7. Avoid casual language/slang. Try: "The viewer's ability to determine the safety of an activity is compromised."

8. Don't address the essay. Avoid phrases like "for example" and "in conclusion." Try: "Participants on "Survivor" have sustained serious injuries as heart attack and burns.

9. Leave yourself time to write a strong conclusion! Try: Designate 3-5 minutes for writing your conclusion.

Common Essay Mistakes - Example 2

Questioning authority makes society stronger. In every aspect our society, there is an authoritative person or group making rules. There is also the group underneath them who are meant to follow. 1 This is true of our country's public schools as well as our federal government. The right to question authority at both of these levels is guaranteed by the United States Declaration of Independence. People are given the ability to question so that authority figures are kept in check 2 and will be forced to listen to the opinions of other people. Questioning authority leads to positive changes in society and preserves what is already working well.

If students never question the authority of a principal's decisions, the best interest of the student body is lost. Good things 3 may not remain in place for the students and no amendment to the rules are sought. Change requires that authority be questioned. An example of this is Silver Head Middle School in Davie, Florida. Last year, the principal felt strongly about enforcing the school's uniform policy. Some students were not bothered by this. 4 Many students felt the policy disregarded their civil rights. A petition voicing student dissatisfaction was signed and presented to the principal. He met with a student representative to discuss the petition. Compromise was reached as a monthly "casual day." The students were able to promote change and peace by questioning authority.

Even at the level of federal government, our country's ultimate authority, the ability to question is the key to the harmony keeping society strong. Most government officials are elected by the public so they have the right to question their authority. 5 If there's a mandate, law, or statement that citizens aren't 6 happy with, they have recourse. Campaigning for or against a political platform and participating in the electoral process give a voice to every opinion. I think elections are very important. 7 Without this questioning and examination of society's laws, the government will represent only the voice of the authority figure. The success of our society is based on the questioning of authority. 8

Society is strengthened by those who question authority. Dialogue is created between people with different visions and change becomes possible. At both the level of public school and of federal government, the positive effects of questioning authority can be witnessed. Whether questioning the decisions of a single principal or the motives of the federal government, it is the willingness of people to question and create change that allows society to grow. A strong society is inspired by many voices, all at different levels. 9 These voices keep society strong.

1. Write concisely. Combine the sentences to improve understanding and cut unnecessary words. Try: "In every aspect of society, there is an authority making rules and a group of people meant to follow them."

2. Avoid slang. Re-word "kept in check." Try: "People are given the ability to question so that authority figures are held accountable and will be forced to listen to the opinions of other people.

2-2. Cut unnecessary words. Try: "People are given the ability to question so that authority figures are held accountable and will listen to other opinions."

3. Use precise language. What are "good things"?Try: "Interesting activities may not remain in place for the students and no amendment to the rules are sought."

Use correct subject-verb agreement. Be careful to identify the correct subject of your sentence. Try: "Interesting activities may not remain in place for the students and no amendment to the rules is sought."

4. Don't add information that doesn't add value to your argument. Cut: "Some students weren't bothered by this."

5. Check for parallel structure. Who has the right to question whose authority? Try: "Having voted them in, the people have the authority to question public officials."

6. Don't use contractions in academic essays. Try: "If there is a mandate, law, or statement that citizens are not happy with, they have recourse."

7. Don't use the pronoun "I" in persuasive essays. Cut opinions. Cut:"I think elections are very important."

8. Use specific examples to prove your argument. Try: Discuss a particular election in depth.

9. Cut redundant sentences. Cut: "A strong society is inspired by many voices, all at different levels."

Writing Concisely

Concise writing is direct and descriptive. The reader follows the writer's thoughts easily. If your writing is concise, a four paragraph essay is acceptable for standardized tests. It's better to write clearly about fewer ideas than to write poorly about many.

This doesn't always mean using fewer words. It means that every word you use is important to the message. Unnecessary or repetitive information dilutes ideas and weakens your writing. The meaning of the word concise comes from the Latin, "to cut up." If it isn't necessary information, don't waste precious testing minutes writing it down.

Being redundant is a quick way to lengthen a sentence or paragraph, but it takes away your power during a timed essay. While many writers use repetition of phrases and key words to make their point, it's important to remove words that don't add value. Redundancy can confuse and lead you away from your subject when you need to write quickly. Be aware that many redundant phrases are part of our daily language and need to be cut from your essay.

For example, "bouquet of flowers" is a redundant phrase as only the word "bouquet" is necessary. Its definition includes flowers. Be especially careful with words you use to stress a point, such as "completely," "totally," and "very."

First of all, I'd like to thank my family.
Revised: First, I'd like to thank my family.

The school *introduced a new* rule.
Revised: The school introduced a rule.

I am *completely full.*
Revised: I am full.

Your glass is *totally empty*!
Revised: Your glass is empty!

Her artwork is *very unique.*
Revised: Her artwork is unique.

Other ways to cut bulk and time include avoiding phrases that have no meaning or power in your essay. Phrases like "in my opinion," "as a matter of fact," and "due to the fact that" are space and time wasters. Also, change passive verbs to active voice.

In my opinion, the paper is well written.
Revised: The paper is well written.

The book *was written* by the best students.
Revised: The best students wrote the book.

The teacher *is listening* to the students.
The teacher listens to the students.

This assigns action to the subject, shortens, and clarifies the sentence. When time is working against you, precise language is on your side.

Not only should you remove redundant phrases, whole sentences without value should be cut too. Replacing general nouns with specific ones is an effective way to accomplish this.

She screamed as the thing came closer. It was a sharp-toothed dog.

Revised: She screamed as the sharp-toothed dog came

closer.

The revised sentence is precise and the paragraph is improved by combining sentences and varying sentence structure. When editing, ask yourself which thoughts should be connected and which need to be separated. Skim each paragraph as you finish writing it and cut as you go.

Leave three to four minutes for final editing. While reading, make a point to pause at every period. This allows you to "hear" sentences the way your reader will, not how you meant them to sound. This will help you find the phrases and sentences that need to be cut or combined. The result is an essay a grader will appreciate.

Redundancy

Duplication and verbosity in English is the use of two or more words that clearly mean the same thing, making one of them unnecessary. It is easy to do use redundant expressions or phrases in a conversation where speech is spontaneous, and common in spoken English. In written English, however, redundancy is more serious and harder to ignore. Here are list of redundant phrases to avoid.

1. Suddenly exploded.

An explosion is instantaneous or immediate and that is sudden enough. No need to use 'suddenly' along with exploded.
2. Final outcome.

An outcome refers to the result. An outcome is intrinsically final and so no need to use final along with outcome.

3. Advance notice/planning/reservations/ warning.

A warning, notice, reservation or plan is made before an event. Once the reader sees any of these words, they know that they were done or carried out before the event. These words do not need to be used with advance.

4. First began, new beginning.

Beginning signals the start or the first time, and therefore the use of "new" is superfluous.
5. Add an additional.

The word 'add' shows the provision of another something, and so "additional" is superfluous.

6. For a period/number of days.

The word "days" is already in plural and clearly signifies more than just one day. It is thus redundant to use "a number of," or "a period of" along with days. Simply state the number of days or of the specific number of days is unknown, you say 'many days.'

7. Foreign imports.

Imports are foreign as they come from another country, so it is superfluous to refer to imports as "foreign."

8. Forever and ever.

Forever indicates eternity and so there is no need for "ever" as it simply duplicated forever.

9. Came at a time when.

"At a time" is not necessary in this phrase because the 'when' already provides a temporal reference to the action, coming.

10. Free gift.

It cannot be a gift if it is paid for. A gift, by nature, is free and so referring to a gift is free is redundant.

11. Collaborate/join/meet/merge together.

The words merge, join, meet and collaborate already suggest people or things coming together. It is unnecessary to use any of these words with together, such as saying merge together or join together. The correct expression is simply to say join or merge, omitting the together.

12. Invited guests.

Guests are those invited for an event. Since they had to be invited to be guests, there is no need to use invited with guests.

13. Major breakthrough.

A breakthrough is significant by nature. It can only be described as a breakthrough when there is a notable progress. The significant nature of the progress is already implied when you use the word "breakthrough," so "major" is redundant.

14. Absolutely certain or sure/essential/ guaranteed.

When someone or something is said to be sure or certain it indicates that it is without doubt. Using "absolutely" in addition to certain or sure is unnecessary. Essential or guaranteed is used for something that is absolute and so also does not need the word absolutely to accompany them.

15. Ask a question.

Ask means to present a question. Using "question" in addition to "ask" is redundant.

16. Basic fundamentals/essentials.

Using basic here is redundant. Essentials and fundamental suggest an elementary nature.

17. [Number] a.m. in the morning/p.m. in the evening.

When you write 8 a.m. the reader knows you mean 8 o'clock in the morning. It is not necessary to say 8 a.m. in the morning. Simply write 8 a.m. or 8 p.m.

18. Definite decision.

A decision is already definite even if it can be reversed later. A decision is a definite course of action has been chosen. No need to use the word definite along with the word decision.

19. Past history/record.

A record or history by definition refers to past events or occurrences. Using past to qualify history or record is unnecessary.

20. Consensus of opinion.

Consensus means agreement over something that may be or not be an opinion. So it may look that using the phrase 'consensus of opinion' is appropriate, but it is better to omit "opinion."

21. Enter in.

Enter means going in, as no one enters out. Therefore no need to add "in," simply use "enter."

22. Plan ahead.

You cannot plan for the past. Planning can only be done for the future. When you use "plan," the future is already implied.

23. Possibly might.
The words might and possibly signify probability, so just use one at a time.

24. Direct confrontation.

A confrontation is a head-on conflict, and does not need to be modified with "direct."

25. Postpone until later.

Something postponed is delayed or moved to a later time, and does not need to be modified with "later."

26. False pretense.

The word pretense is only used to describe a deception, so a "false" pretense is redundant.

27. Protest against.

Protest involves showing opposition; there is no need to use against.

28. End result.

Result only comes at the end. The reader who sees the word 'result' already knows that it occurs at the end.

29. Estimated at about/roughly.

Estimates are approximations that are not expected to be accurate, and do not need to be modified with "roughly" or "about."

30. Repeat again.

Repeat refers to something done again and does not need to be modified with "again."

31. Difficult dilemma.

A dilemma is a situation that is complicated or difficult, and does not need to be modified with "difficult."

32. Revert back.

Revert indicates returning to a former or earlier state. Something that reverts goes back to how it used to be. No need to add back.

33. (During the) course (of).

During means "in or throughout the duration of," and doesn't require the use of the word "course."

34. Same identical.

Same and identical means the same thing and should not be used together.

35. Completely filled/finished/opposite.

Completely indicates thoroughness. However, the words finished and filled already indicate something thoroughly filled or finished to the extent possible. The words filled and finished thus do not need to be qualified with "completely."

36. Since the time when.

In this phrase, 'the time when' is not necessary as 'since' already indicates sometime in the past.

37. Close proximity/scrutiny.

Proximity means being close, in respect to location. Scrutiny means studying something closely. Both words already suggest close, whether in respect to location as with proximity, or in respect to study, as with scrutiny. It is therefore unnecessary to use the words together.

38. Spell out in detail.

'Spell out' involves providing details, so no need to add "in detail."

39. Written down.

Anything written can be said to be taken down. Written should therefore be used on its own.

40. (Filled to) capacity.

Anything that is filled has reached its capacity and so the word capacity does not need to be used along with filled.

41. Unintended mistake.

Something is a mistake because it is not intended. The lack of intention is plain and so there is no need to qualify with "unintended."

42. Still remains.

"Remains" signifies that something is still as it is, and so using 'still' is superfluous.

43. Actual experience/fact.

Something becomes an experience after it has occurred. If it didn't occur it is not an experience. A fact can only be a fact when it is sure or confirmed. Both experience and fact thus do not need to be modified with "actual."

44. Therapeutic treatment.

Therapeutic refers to the healing or curing of illness. By nature all medical treatment is therapeutic in that it aims to heal or cure. When speaking of medical treatment, there is thus no need to use therapeutic to qualify treatment.

45. At the present time.

"At present" alone indicates the present time or "at this

time." Using "at the present time" is the verbose version. Better to just use "at present."

46. Unexpected surprise.

A surprise is unexpected by nature. The unexpected nature is assumed once the word surprised is read or heard. No need to use unexpected to qualify it.

47. As for example.

"As" indicates the use of an example and so it is redundant to say "an example."

48. Usual custom.

A custom refers to something that is observed or done re-peatedly or routinely. The use of 'usual' along with custom is not necessary.

49. Added bonus.

Bonus already indicates something extra, in addition to the ordinary. Using "added" to describe the bonus is not neces-sary.

50. Few in number.

Something is few because it is small in number. No need to use number with few.

Practice Test Questions Set 1

The questions below are not the same as you will find on the Accuplacer® - that would be too easy! And nobody knows what the questions will be and they change all the time. Below are general questions that cover the same subject areas as the Accuplacer®. So, while the format and exact wording of the questions may differ slightly, and change from year to year, if you can answer the questions below, you will have no problem with the Accuplacer®.

For the best results, take these practice test questions as if it were the real exam. Set aside time when you will not be disturbed, and a location that is quiet and free of distractions. Read the instructions carefully, read each question carefully, and answer to the best of your ability.
Use the bubble answer sheets provided. When you have completed the practice questions, check your answer against the Answer Key and read the explanation provided.

Do not attempt more than one set of practice test questions in one day. After completing the first practice test, wait two or three days before attempting the second set of questions.

Reading Answer Sheet

1. (A) (B) (C) (D)   11. (A) (B) (C) (D)   21. (A) (B) (C) (D)

2. (A) (B) (C) (D)   12. (A) (B) (C) (D)   22. (A) (B) (C) (D)

3. (A) (B) (C) (D)   13. (A) (B) (C) (D)   23. (A) (B) (C) (D)

4. (A) (B) (C) (D)   14. (A) (B) (C) (D)   24. (A) (B) (C) (D)

5. (A) (B) (C) (D)   15. (A) (B) (C) (D)   25. (A) (B) (C) (D)

6. (A) (B) (C) (D)   16. (A) (B) (C) (D)   26. (A) (B) (C) (D)

7. (A) (B) (C) (D)   17. (A) (B) (C) (D)   27. (A) (B) (C) (D)

8. (A) (B) (C) (D)   18. (A) (B) (C) (D)   28. (A) (B) (C) (D)

9. (A) (B) (C) (D)   19. (A) (B) (C) (D)   29. (A) (B) (C) (D)

10. (A) (B) (C) (D)   20. (A) (B) (C) (D)   30. (A) (B) (C) (D)

Mathematics Answer Sheet
(Arithmetic, Algebra and College Level Math)

1. (A) (B) (C) (D)	21. (A) (B) (C) (D)	41. (A) (B) (C) (D)
2. (A) (B) (C) (D)	22. (A) (B) (C) (D)	42. (A) (B) (C) (D)
3. (A) (B) (C) (D)	23. (A) (B) (C) (D)	43. (A) (B) (C) (D)
4. (A) (B) (C) (D)	24. (A) (B) (C) (D)	44. (A) (B) (C) (D)
5. (A) (B) (C) (D)	25. (A) (B) (C) (D)	45. (A) (B) (C) (D)
6. (A) (B) (C) (D)	26. (A) (B) (C) (D)	46. (A) (B) (C) (D)
7. (A) (B) (C) (D)	27. (A) (B) (C) (D)	47. (A) (B) (C) (D)
8. (A) (B) (C) (D)	28. (A) (B) (C) (D)	48. (A) (B) (C) (D)
9. (A) (B) (C) (D)	29. (A) (B) (C) (D)	49. (A) (B) (C) (D)
10. (A) (B) (C) (D)	30. (A) (B) (C) (D)	50. (A) (B) (C) (D)
11. (A) (B) (C) (D)	31. (A) (B) (C) (D)	51. (A) (B) (C) (D)
12. (A) (B) (C) (D)	32. (A) (B) (C) (D)	52. (A) (B) (C) (D)
13. (A) (B) (C) (D)	33. (A) (B) (C) (D)	53. (A) (B) (C) (D)
14. (A) (B) (C) (D)	34. (A) (B) (C) (D)	54. (A) (B) (C) (D)
15. (A) (B) (C) (D)	35. (A) (B) (C) (D)	55. (A) (B) (C) (D)
16. (A) (B) (C) (D)	36. (A) (B) (C) (D)	56. (A) (B) (C) (D)
17. (A) (B) (C) (D)	37. (A) (B) (C) (D)	57. (A) (B) (C) (D)
18. (A) (B) (C) (D)	38. (A) (B) (C) (D)	58. (A) (B) (C) (D)
19. (A) (B) (C) (D)	39. (A) (B) (C) (D)	59. (A) (B) (C) (D)
20. (A) (B) (C) (D)	40. (A) (B) (C) (D)	60. (A) (B) (C) (D)

Sentence Skills Answer Sheet

1. (A) (B) (C) (D)   11. (A) (B) (C) (D)

2. (A) (B) (C) (D)   12. (A) (B) (C) (D)

3. (A) (B) (C) (D)   13. (A) (B) (C) (D)

4. (A) (B) (C) (D)   14. (A) (B) (C) (D)

5. (A) (B) (C) (D)   15. (A) (B) (C) (D)

6. (A) (B) (C) (D)   16. (A) (B) (C) (D)

7. (A) (B) (C) (D)   17. (A) (B) (C) (D)

8. (A) (B) (C) (D)   18. (A) (B) (C) (D)

9. (A) (B) (C) (D)   19. (A) (B) (C) (D)

10. (A) (B) (C) (D)   20. (A) (B) (C) (D)

Part 1 - Reading

Questions 1 – 4 refer to the following passage.

The Life of Helen Keller

Many people have heard of Helen Keller. She is famous because she was unable to see or hear, but learned to speak and read and went onto attend college and earn a degree. Her life is a very interesting story, one that she developed into an autobiography, which was then adapted into both a stage play and a movie. How did Helen Keller overcome her disabilities to become a famous woman? Read onto find out. Helen Keller was not born blind and deaf. When she was a small baby, she had a very high fever for several days. As a result of her sudden illness, baby Helen lost her eyesight and her hearing. Because she was so young when she went deaf and blind, Helen Keller never had any recollection of being able to see or hear. Since she could not hear, she could not learn to talk. Since she could not see, it was difficult for her to move around. For the first six years of her life, her world was very still and dark.

Imagine what Helen's childhood must have been like. She could not hear her mother's voice. She could not see the beauty of her parent's farm. She could not recognize who was giving her a hug, or a bath or even where her bedroom was each night. More sad, she could not communicate with her parents in any way. She could not express her feelings or tell them the things she wanted. It must have been a very sad childhood.

When Helen was six years old, her parents hired her a teacher named Anne Sullivan. Anne was a young woman who was almost blind. However, she could hear and she could read Braille, so she was a perfect teacher for young Helen. At first, Anne had a very hard time teaching Helen anything. She described her first impression of Helen as a "wild thing, not a child." Helen did not like Anne at first either. She bit and hit Anne when Anne tried to teach her. However, the two of them eventually came to have a great deal of love and respect.

Anne taught Helen to hear by putting her hands on people's throats. She could feel the sounds that people made. In time, Helen learned to feel what people said. Next, Anne taught Helen to read Braille, which is a way that books are written for the blind. Finally, Anne taught Helen to talk. Although Helen did learn to talk, it was hard for anyone but Anne to understand her.

As Helen grew older, more and more people were amazed by her story. She went to college and wrote books about her life. She gave talks to the public, with Anne at her side, translating her words. Today, both Anne Sullivan and Helen Keller are famous women who are respected for their lives' work.

1. Helen Keller could not see and hear and so, what was her biggest problem in childhood?

     a. Inability to communicate

     b. Inability to walk

     c. Inability to play

     d. Inability to eat

2. Helen learned to hear by feeling the vibrations people made when they spoke. What were these vibrations were felt through?

     a. Mouth

     b. Throat

     c. Ears

     d. Lips

3. From the passage, we can infer that Anne Sullivan was a patient teacher. We can infer this because

a. Helen hit and bit her and Anne still remained her teacher.

b. Anne taught Helen to read only.

c. Anne was hard of hearing too.

d. Anne wanted to be a teacher.

4. Helen Keller learned to speak but Anne translated her words when she spoke in public. The reason Helen needed a translator was because

a. Helen spoke another language.

b. Helen's words were hard for people to understand.

c. Helen spoke very quietly.

d. Helen did not speak but only used sign language.

Questions 5 – 7 refer to the following passage.

Thunderstorms

The first stage of a thunderstorm is the cumulus stage, or developing stage. In this stage, masses of moisture are lifted upwards into the atmosphere. The trigger for this lift can be insulation heating the ground producing thermals, areas where two winds converge, forcing air upwards, or, where winds blow over terrain of increasing elevation. Moisture in the air rapidly cools into liquid drops of water, which appears as cumulus clouds.

As the water vapor condenses into liquid, latent heat is released which warms the air, causing it to become less dense than the surrounding dry air. The warm air rises in an updraft through the process of convection (hence the term convective precipitation). This creates a low-pressure zone beneath the forming thunderstorm. In a typical thunderstorm, about 5×10^8 kg of water vapor is lifted, and the quantity of energy released when this condenses is about equal to the energy used by a city of 100,000 in a month. [1]

5. The cumulus stage of a thunderstorm is the

    a. The last stage of the storm.

    b. The middle stage of the storm formation.

    c. The beginning of the thunderstorm.

    d. The period after the thunderstorm has ended.

6. One of the ways the air is warmed is

    a. Air moving downwards, which creates a high-pressure zone.

    b. Air cooling and becoming less dense, causing it to rise.

    c. Moisture moving downward toward the earth.

    d. Heat created by water vapor condensing into liquid.

7. Identify the correct sequence of events.

    a. Warm air rises, water droplets condense, creating more heat, and the air rises farther.

    b. Warm air rises and cools, water droplets condense, causing low pressure.

    c. Warm air rises and collects water vapor, the water vapor condenses as the air rises, which creates heat, and causes the air to rise farther.

    d. None of the above.

Questions 8 – 10 refer to the following passage.

What Is Mardi Gras?

Mardi Gras is fast becoming one of the South's most famous and most celebrated holidays. The word Mardi Gras comes from the French and the literal translation is "Fat Tuesday." The holiday has also been called Shrove Tuesday, due to its associations with Lent. The purpose of Mardi Gras is to celebrate and enjoy before the Lenten season of fasting and repentance begins.

What originated by the French Explorers in New Orleans, Louisiana in the 17th century is now celebrated all over the world. Panama, Italy, Belgium and Brazil all host large scale Mardi Gras celebrations, and many smaller cities and towns celebrate this fun loving Tuesday as well. Usually held in February or early March, Mardi Gras is a day of extravagance, a day for people to eat, drink and be merry, to wear costumes, masks and to dance to jazz music.
The French explorers on the Mississippi River would be in shock today if they saw the opulence of the parades and floats that grace the New Orleans streets during Mardi Gras these days. Parades in New Orleans are divided by organizations. These are more commonly known as Krewes.

Being a member of a Krewe is quite a task because Krewes are responsible for overseeing the parades. Each Krewe's parade is ruled by a Mardi Gras "King and Queen." The role of the King and Queen is to "bestow" gifts on their adoring fans as the floats ride along the street. They throw doubloons, which is fake money and usually colored green, purple and gold, which are the colors of Mardi Gras. Beads in those color shades are also thrown and cups are thrown as well. Beads are by far the most popular souvenir of any Mardi Gras parade, with each spectator attempting to gather as many as possible.

8. The purpose of Mardi Gras is to

    a. Repent for a month.

    b. Celebrate in extravagant ways.

    c. Be a member of a Krewe.

    d. Explore the Mississippi.

9. From reading the passage we can infer that "Kings and Queens"

    a. Have to be members of a Krewe.

    b. Have to be French.

    c. Have to know how to speak French.

    d. Have to give away their own money.

10. Which group of people first began to hold Mardi Gras celebrations?

    a. Settlers from Italy

    b. Members of Krewes

    c. French explorers

    d. Belgium explorers

Questions 11 – 13 refer to the following passage.

Clouds

A cloud is a visible mass of droplets or frozen crystals floating in the atmosphere above the surface of the Earth or other planetary bodies. Another type of cloud is a mass of material in space, attracted by gravity, called interstellar clouds and nebulae. The branch of meteorology which studies clouds is called nephrology. When we are speaking of Earth clouds, water vapor is usually the condensing substance, which forms small droplets or ice crystal. These crystals are typically 0.01 mm in diameter. Dense, deep clouds reflect most light, so they appear white, at least from the top. Cloud droplets scatter light very efficiently, so the farther into a cloud light travels, the weaker it gets. This accounts for the gray or dark appearance at the base of large clouds. Thin clouds may appear to have acquired the color of their environment or background. [2]

11. What are clouds made of?

   a. Water droplets

   b. Ice crystals

   c. Ice crystals and water droplets

   d. Clouds on Earth are made of ice crystals and water droplets

12. The main idea of this passage is

   a. Condensation occurs in clouds, having an intense effect on the weather on the surface of the earth.

   b. Atmospheric gases are responsible for the gray color of clouds just before a severe storm happens.

   c. A cloud is a visible mass of droplets or frozen crystals floating in the atmosphere above the surface of the Earth or other planetary body.

   d. Clouds reflect light in varying amounts and degrees, depending on the size and concentration of the water droplets.

13. Why are clouds white on top and grey on the bottom?

   a. Because water droplets inside the cloud do not reflect light, it appears white, and the farther into the cloud the light travels, the less light is reflected making the bottom appear dark.

   b. Because water droplets outside the cloud reflect light, it appears dark, and the farther into the cloud the light travels, the more light is reflected making the bottom appear white.

   c. Because water droplets inside the cloud reflects light, making it appear white, and the farther into the cloud the light travels, the more light is reflected making the bottom appear dark.

   d. None of the above.

Questions 14 - 17 refer to the following passage.

Keeping Tropical Fish

Keeping tropical fish at home or in your office used to be very popular. Today, interest has declined, but it remains as rewarding and relaxing a hobby as ever. Ask any tropical fish hobbyist, and you will hear how soothing and relaxing watching colorful fish live their lives in the aquarium. If you are considering keeping tropical fish as pets, here is a list of the basic equipment you will need.

A filter is essential for keeping your aquarium clean and your fish alive and healthy. There are different types and sizes of filters and the right size for you depends on the size of the aquarium and the level of stocking. Generally, you need a filter with a 3 to 5 times turn over rate per hour. This means that the water in the tank should go through the filter about 3 to 5 times per hour.

Most tropical fish do well in water temperatures ranging between 24^0C and 26^0C, though each has its own ideal water temperature. A heater with a thermostat is necessary to regulate the water temperature. Some heaters are submersible and others are not, so check carefully before you buy. Lights are also necessary, and come in a large variety of types, strengths and sizes. A light source is necessary for plants in the tank to photosynthesize and give the tank a more attractive appearance. Even if you plan to use plastic plants, the fish still require light, although here you can use a lower strength light source.

A hood is necessary to keep dust, dirt and unwanted materials out of the tank. Sometimes the hood can also help prevent evaporation. Another requirement is aquarium gravel. This will improve the aesthetics of the aquarium and is necessary if you plan to have real plants.

14. What is the general tone of this article?

   a. Formal

   b. Informal

   c. Technical

   d. Opinion

15. Which of the following cannot be inferred?

   a. Gravel is good for aquarium plants.

   b. Fewer people have aquariums in their office than at home.

   c. The larger the tank, the larger the filter required.

   d. None of the above.

16. What evidence does the author provide to support their claim that aquarium lights are necessary?

   a. Plants require light.

   b. Fish and plants require light.

   c. The author does not provide evidence for this statement.

   d. Aquarium lights make the aquarium more attractive.

17. Which of the following is an opinion?

   a. Filter with a 3 to 5 times turn over rate per hour are required.

   b. Aquarium gravel improves the aesthetics of the aquarium.

   c. An aquarium hood keeps dust, dirt and unwanted materials out of the tank.

   d. Each type of tropical fish has its own ideal water temperature.

Questions 18 - 20 refer to the following passage.

Ways Characters Communicate in Theater

Playwrights give their characters voices in a way that gives depth and added meaning to what happens on stage during their play. There are different types of speech in scripts that allow characters to talk with themselves, with other characters, and even with the audience.

It is very unique to theater that characters may talk "to themselves." When characters do this, the speech they give is called a soliloquy. Soliloquies are usually poetic, introspective, moving, and can tell audience members about the feelings, motivations, or suspicions of an individual character without that character having to reveal them to other characters on stage. "To be or not to be" is a famous soliloquy given by Hamlet as he considers difficult but important themes, such as life and death.

The most common type of communication in plays is when one character is speaking to another or a group of other characters. This is generally called dialogue, but can also be called monologue if one character speaks without being interrupted for a long time. It is not necessarily the most important type of communication, but it is the most common because the plot of the play cannot really progress without it.

Lastly, and most unique to theater (although it has been used somewhat in film) is when a character speaks directly to the audience. This is called an aside, and scripts usually specifically direct actors to do this. Asides are usually comical, an inside joke between the character and the audience, and very short. The actor will usually face the audience when delivering them, even if it's for a moment, so the audience can recognize this move as an aside.

All three of these types of communication are important to the art of theater, and have been perfected by famous playwrights like Shakespeare. Understanding these types of communication can help an audience member grasp what is artful about the script and action of a play.

18. According to the passage, characters in plays communicate to

a. move the plot forward

b. show the private thoughts and feelings of one character

c. make the audience laugh

d. add beauty and artistry to the play

19. When Hamlet delivers "To be or not to be," he can most likely be described as

a. solitary

b. thoughtful

c. dramatic

d. hopeless

20. The author uses parentheses to punctuate "although it has been used somewhat in film"

a. to show that films are less important

b. instead of using commas so that the sentence is not interrupted

c. because parenthesis help separate details that are not as important

d. to show that films are not as artistic

Instructions: For each of the questions below, you are given 2 sentences, followed by a question about the relationship between the 2 sentences. Choose the best answer that describes the relationship.

21. An example of a cold-blooded animal that hibernates underground during the winter is the snake.

Snakes, such as garter snakes and western rattlesnakes, hibernate underground in large groups during the winter.

    a. The second sentence reinforces the first.

    b. The second sentence analyzes a statement made in the first.

    c. The second sentence proposes a solution.

    d. The second sentence draws a conclusion.

22. The dog barked and ran.

The dog barked and ran after the postman who was delivering mail.

    a. The second sentence analyzes a statement made in the first.

    b. The second sentence reinforces the first.

    c. The second sentence expands on the first.

    d. The second sentence proposes a solution.

24. Aphids, pest commonly found on roses, are destroying my rose bushes.

If I spray my rose bushes with insecticidal soap, I will kill the aphids.

    a. The second sentence draws a conclusion.

    b. The second sentence reinforces the first.

    c. The second sentence analyzes a statement made in the first.

    d. The second sentence proposes a solution.

25. Ms. Apple received and reviewed her students', who all scored on the 99th percentile on the standardized test.

She discovered that most of her students performed at the highest level of achievement; thus, they mastered the material and skills taught.

    a. The second sentence reinforces the first.

    b. The second sentence proposes a solution.

    c. The second sentence analyzes a statement made in the first.

    d. The second sentence expands on the first.

26. Human activities have contributed to global warming.

Due to global warming, hurricanes, tornadoes and other storms will become stronger and more frequent.

    a. The second sentence contrasts the first.

    b. The second sentence restates an idea in the first sentence.

    c. The second sentence states an effect.

    d. The second sentence gives an example.

27. Jungles and rainforests are both associated with tropical climates.

Vegetation in jungles are tangled and impenetrable (hard to walk through without cutting your way through); however, vegetation in the rainforest is sparse.

    a. The second sentence restates an idea in the first sentence.

    b. The second sentence states an effect.

    c. The second sentence gives an example.

    d. The second sentence contrasts the first.

28. Rosaline's friend invited her to the Civil Rights Photography Exhibit at the local museum.

Rosaline did not know as much as she wanted to about the African-American Civil Rights Movement, so she went to the library and checked out books related to the African-American Civil Rights Movement.

    a. They repeat the same idea.

    b. They provide a problem and solution.

    c. They contradict each other.

    d. They reinforce each other.

29. Parrots and macaws are beautiful, colorful birds.

There are over 370 species of parrots, but there are only 18 species of macaws.

    a. They establish a contrast.

    b. They provide a problem and solution.

    c. They contradict each other.

    d. They reinforce each other.

30. Paris is often referred to as the "City of Lights."

Paris is called the "City of Lights" because there are over 296 illuminated sites and buildings in Paris, and most importantly, Paris was the birthplace of the Age of Enlightenment.

    a. They establish a contrast.

    b. They reinforce each other.

    c. They provide a problem and solution.

    d. They contradict each other.

Arithmetic

1. Brad has agreed to buy everyone a Coke. Each drink costs $1.89, and there are 5 friends. Estimate Brad's cost.

    a. $7

    b. $8

    c. $10

    d. $12

2. c = 4, n = 5 and x = 3. then 2cnx/2n =?

    a. 12

    b. 50

    c. 8

    d. 21

3. What fraction of $1500 is $75?

    a. 1/14

    b. 3/5

    c. 7/10

    d. 1/20

4. Estimate 16 x 230.

    a. 31,000

    b. 301,000

    c. 3,100

    d. 3,000,000

5. Below is the attendance for a class of 45.

Day	Number of Absent Students
Monday	5
Tuesday	9
Wednesday	4
Thursday	10
Friday	6

What is the average attendance for the week?

    a. 88%

    b. 85%

    c. 81%

    d. 77%

6. John purchased a jacket at a 7% discount. He had a membership which gave him an additional 2% discount on the discounted price. If he paid $425, what is the retail price of the jacket?

    a. $460

    b. $466

    c. $466

    d. $472

7. Estimate 215 x 65.

    a. 1,350

    b. 13,500

    c. 103,500

    d. 3,500

8. 10 x 2 – (7 + 9)

    a. 21

    b. 16

    c. 4

    d. 13

9. 40% of a number is equal to 90. What is the half of the number?

    a. 18

    b. 112.5

    c. 225

    d. 120

10. 1/4 + 3/10 =

    a. 9/10

    b. 11/20

    c. 7/15

    d. 3/40

11. A map uses a scale of 1:2,000   How much distance on the ground is 5.2 inches on the map if the scale is in inches?

    a. 100,400

    b. 10,500

    c. 10,400

    d. 1,400

12. A shop sells a piece of industrial equipment for $545. If 15% of the cost was added to the price as value added tax, what is the actual cost of the equipment?

    a. $490.40

    b. $473.91

    c. $505.00

    d. $503.15

13. What is 0.27 + 0.33 expressed as a fraction?

    a. 3/6

    b. 4/7

    c. 3/5

    d. 2/7

14. 5 men have to share a load weighing 10 kg 550 g equally among themselves. How much weight will each man have to carry?

    a. 900 g

    b. 1.5 kg

    c. 3 kg

    d. 2 kg 110 g

15. 1/4 + 11/16

    a. 9/16

    b. 1 1/16

    c. 11/16

    d. 15/12

16. A square lawn has an area of 62,500 square meters. What is the cost of building fence around it at a rate of $5.5 per meter?

   a. $4,000

   b. $5,500

   c. $4,500

   d. $5,000

17. A mother is 7 times older than her child. In 25 years, her age will be double that of her child. How old is the mother now?

   a. 35

   b. 33

   c. 30

   d. 25

18. Convert 0.28 to a fraction.

   a. 7/25

   b. 3.25

   c. 8/25

   d. 5/28

19. If a discount of 20% is given for a desk and Mark saves $45, how much did he pay for the desk?

   a. $225

   b. $160

   c. $180

   d. $210

20. In a grade 8 exam, students are asked to divide a number by 3/2, but a student mistakenly multiplied the number by 3/2 and the answer is 5 more than the required one. What was the number?

    a. 4

    b. 5

    c. 6

    d. 8

Algebra

21. Divide 243 by 3^3

    a. 243

    b. 11

    c. 9

    d. 27

22. Solve the following equation $4(y + 6) = 3y + 30$

    a. $y = 20$

    b. $y = 6$

    c. $y = 30/7$

    d. $y = 30$

23. Divide $x^2 - y^2$ by $x - y$.

    a. $x - y$

    b. $x + y$

    c. xy

    d. $y - x$

24. Solve for x if, 10^2 x $100^2 = 1000^x$

    a. x = 2

    b. x = 3

    c. x = -2

    d. x = 0

25. Given polynomials A = $-2x^4 + x^2 - 3x$, B = $x^4 - x^3 + 5$ and C = $x^4 + 2x^3 + 4x + 5$, find A + B - C.

    a. $x^3 + x^2 + x + 10$

    b. $-3x^3 + x^2 - 7x + 10$

    c. $-2x^4 - 3x^3 + x^2 - 7x$

    d. $-3x^4 + x^3 + 2 - 7x$

26. Solve the inequality: $(x - 6)^2 \geq x^2 + 12$

    a. $[2, + \infty)$

    b. $(2, + \infty)$

    c. $(-\infty, 2]$

    d. $(12, + \infty)$

27. $7^5 - 3^5$ =

    a. 15,000

    b. 16,564

    c. 15,800

    d. 15,007

28. Divide $x^3 - 3x^2 + 3x - 1$ by x - 1.

    a. $x^2 - 1$

    b. $x^2 + 1$

    c. $x^2 - 2x + 1$

    d. $x^2 + 2x + 1$

29. Express 9 x 9 x 9 in exponential form and standard form.

    a. $9^3 = 719$

    b. $9^3 = 629$

    c. $9^3 = 729$

    d. $10^3 = 729$

30. Using the factoring method, solve the quadratic equation: $x^2 - 5x - 6 = 0$

    a. -6 and 1

    b. -1 and 6

    c. 1 and 6

    d. -6 and -1

31. Divide 0.524 by 10^3

    a. 0.0524

    b. 0.000524

    c. 0.00524

    d. 524

32. Factor the polynomial $x^3y^3 - x^2y^8$.

    a. $x^2y^3(x - y^5)$

    b. $x^3y^3(1 - y^5)$

    c. $x^2y^2(x - y^6)$

    d. $xy^3(x - y^5)$

33. Find the solution for the following linear equation: $5x/2 = (3x + 24)/6$.

    a. -1

    b. 0

    c. 1

    d. 2

34. 3^2 x 3^5

    a. 3^{17}

    b. 3^5

    c. 4^8

    d. 3^7

35. Solve the system, if a is some real number:

ax + y = 1
x + ay = 1

    a. (1,a)

    b. (1/a + 1, 1)

    c. (1/(a + 1), 1/(a + 1))

    d. (a, 1/a + 1)

36. Solve $3^5 \div 3^8$

    a. 3^3

    b. 3^5

    c. 3^6

    d. 3^1

37. Solve the linear equation: 3(x + 2) - 2(1 - x) = 4x + 5

    a. -1

    b. 0

    c. 1

    d. 2

38. Simplify the following expression: $3x^a + 6a^x - x^a + (-5a^x) - 2x^a$

    a. $a^x + x^a$

    b. $a^x - x^a$

    c. a^x

    d. x^a

39. Add polynomials $-3x^2 + 2x + 6$ and $-x^2 - x - 1$.

    a. $-2x^2 + x + 5$

    b. $-4x^2 + x + 5$

    c. $-2x^2 + 3x + 5$

    d. $-4x^2 + 3x + 5$

40. 10^4 is not equal to which of the following?

    a. $100,000$

    b. $10 \times 10 \times 10 \times 10$

    c. $10^2 \times 10^2$

    d. $10,000$

College Level

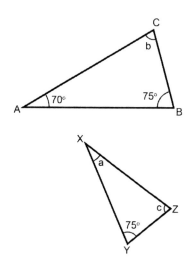

41. What are the respective values of a, b & c if both triangles are similar?

  a. 70°, 70°, 35°

  b. 70°, 35°, 70°

  c. 35°, 35°, 35°

  d. 70°, 35°, 35°

42. For what x is the following equation correct:

$$\log_x 125 = 3$$

  a. 1

  b. 2

  c. 3

  d. 5

43. What is the value of the expression $(1 - 4\sin^2(\pi/6))/(1 + 4\cos^2(\pi/3))$?

    a. -2

    b. -1

    c. 0

    d. 1/2

44. Calculate $(\sin^2 30° - \sin 0°)/(\cos 90° - \cos 60°)$.

    a. -1/2

    b. 2/3

    c. 0

    d. 1/2

45. Consider 2 triangles, ABC and A'B'C', where:

BC = B' C'

AC = A' C'

RA = RA'

Are these 2 triangles congruent?

    a. Yes

    b. No

    c. Not enough information

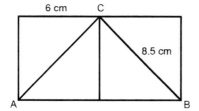

Note: Figure not drawn to scale

46. Assuming the 2 quadrangles are identical rectangles, what is the perimeter of △ABC in the above shape?

    a. 25.5 cm

    b. 27 cm

    c. 30 cm

    d. 29 cm

47. Find the cotangent of a right angle.

    a. -1

    b. 0

    c. 1/2

    d. -1/2

48. If angle α is equal to the expression 3π/2 - π/6 - π - π/3, find sinα.

    a. 0

    b. 1/2

    c. 1

    d. 3/2

49. Find x if $\log_x(9/25) = 2$.

    a. 3/5

    b. 5/3

    c. 6/5

    d. 5/6

50. If $a_0 = 1/2$ and $an = 2a_{n-1}^2$, find a_2 of the sequence $\{a_n\}$.

    a. 1/2

    b. 1/4

    c. 1/16

    d. 1/24

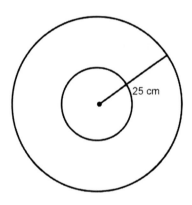

Note: figure not drawn to scale

51. What is the distance travelled by the wheel above, when it makes 175 revolutions?

    a. 87.5 π m

    b. 875 π m

    c. 8.75 π m

    d. 8750 π m

52. If members of the sequence $\{a_n\}$ are represented by $a_n = (-1)^n a_{n-1}$ and if $a_2 = 2$, find a_0.

    a. 2

    b. 1

    c. 0

    d. -2

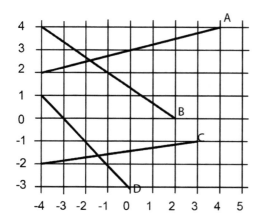

53. Which of the lines above represents the equation $2y - x = 4$?

    a. A

    b. B

    c. C

    d. D

54. For any α, find tgα•ctgα.

    a. -1

    b. 0

    c. 1/2

    d. 1

55. If cosα = 3/5 and b = 24, find side c.

    a. 25

    b. 30

    c. 35

    d. 40

56. Find the sides of a right triangle whose sides are consecutive numbers.

    a. 1, 2, 3

    b. 2, 3, 4

    c. 3, 4, 5

    d. 4, 5, 6

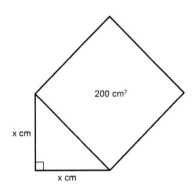

Note: figure not drawn to scale

57. Assuming the quadrangle is square, what is the length of the sides in the triangle above?

    a. 10

    b. 20

    c. 100

    d. 40

58. Calculate (cos(π/2) + ctg(π/2))/sin(π/2).

    a. -2

    b. -1

    c. 0

    d. 1/2

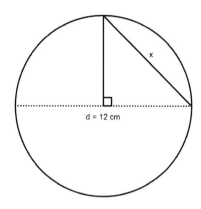

d = 12 cm

Note: figure not drawn to scale

59. Calculate the length of side x.

    a. 6.46

    b. 8.48

    c. 3.6

    d. 6.4

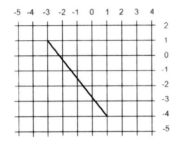

60. What is the slope of the line shown above?

    a. 5/4

    b. -4/5

    c. -5/4

    d. -4/5

Sentence Skills

Directions: Select the best option to replace the underlined portion of the sentence.

1. If Joe had told me the truth, <u>I wouldn't have been</u> so angry.

    a. No change is necessary

    b. If Joe would have told me the truth, I wouldn't have been so angry.

    c. I wouldn't have been so angry if Joe would have told the truth.

    d. If Joe would have telled me the truth, I wouldn't have been so angry.

2. Although you may <u>not see nobody in the dark, it does</u> <u>not mean that not nobody</u> is there.

    a. Although you may not see nobody in the dark, it does not mean that nobody is there.

    b. Although you may not see anyone in the dark, it does not mean that not nobody is there.

    c. Although you may not see anyone in the dark, it does not mean that anyone is there.

    d. No change is necessary.

3. The Ford Motor Company was named for Henry Ford, <u>whom</u> had founded the company.

    a. The Ford Motor Company was named for Henry Ford, which had founded the company.

    b. The Ford Motor Company was named for Henry Ford, who founded the company.

    c. The Ford Motor Company was named for Henry Ford, whose had founded the company.

    d. No change is necessary.

4. Thomas Edison <u>will had been known</u> as the greatest inventor since he invented the light bulb, television, motion pictures, and phonograph.

    a. Thomas Edison has always been known as the greatest inventor since he invented the light bulb, television, motion pictures, and phonograph.

    b. Thomas Edison was always been known as the greatest inventor since he invented the light bulb, television, motion pictures, and phonograph.

    c. Thomas Edison must have had been always known as the greatest inventor since he invented the light bulb, television, motion pictures, and phonograph.

    d. No change is necessary.

5. The weatherman on Channel 6 said that this has been the hottest summer on record.

    a. The weatherman on Channel 6 said that this has been the most hotter summer on record

    b. The weatherman on Channel 6 said that this has been the most hottest summer on record

    c. The weatherman on Channel 6 said that this has been the hotter summer on record

    d. No change is necessary.

6. Although Joe is tall for his age, his brother Elliot is the tallest of the two.

    a. Although Joe is tall for his age, his brother Elliot is more tallest of the two.

    b. Although Joe is tall for his age, his brother Elliot is the tall the two.

    c. Although Joe is tall for his age, his brother Elliot is the taller of the two.

    d. No change is necessary

7. When KISS came to town, all the tickets was sold out before I could buy one.

    a. When KISS came to town, all the tickets will be sold out before I could buy one.

    b. When KISS came to town, all the tickets had been sold out before I could buy one.

    c. When KISS came to town, all the tickets were being sold out before I could buy one.

    d. No change is necessary.

8. The rules of most sports <u>has been</u> more complicated than we often realize.

> a. The rules of most sports are more complicated than we often realize.
>
> b. The rules of most sports is more complicated than we often realize.
>
> c. The rules of most sports was more complicated than we often realize.
>
> d. No change is necessary.

9. Neither of the Wright Brothers <u>had any doubts</u> that they would be successful with their flying machine.

> a. Neither of the Wright Brothers have any doubts that they would be successful with their flying machine.
>
> b. Neither of the Wright Brothers has any doubts that they would be successful with their flying machine.
>
> c. Neither of the Wright Brothers had any doubts that they would be successful with their flying machine.
>
> d. No change is necessary.

10. The Titanic <u>has already sunk</u> mere days into its maiden voyage.

> a. The Titanic will already sunk mere days into its maiden voyage.
>
> b. The Titanic already sank mere days into its maiden voyage.
>
> c. The Titanic sank mere days into its maiden voyage.
>
> d. No change is necessary.

11. The second act was followed by an intermission.

Rewrite, beginning with

An intermission

The next words will be

    a. came after the second act

    b. was followed by the second act

    c. following the second act

    d. came before the second act

12. As he was boarding the plane, Thomas discovered that he had forgotten his toothbrush.

Rewrite, beginning with

Thomas was boarding the plane

The next words will be

    a. as he was discovering

    b. as he had forgotten

    c. when he forgot

    d. when he discovered

13. Because of the wild coyotes, they built a fence for their puppy.

Rewrite, beginning with

They built a fence

The next words will be

    a. because of the puppy

    b. to protect their puppy from

    c. for their wild coyote

    d. because to protect

14. The more time you invest in learning a second language, the more enjoyable it becomes.

Rewrite, beginning with

Learning a second language becomes more enjoyable

The next words will be

    a. the more investing

    b. as you invest more

    c. and the more you

    d. but you invest more

15. It is annoying, but necessary to own a cell phone.

Rewrite, beginning with

While necessary,

The next words will be

    a. it is annoying to

    b. but owning a cell phone

    c. owning a cell phone

    d. cell phones are

16. The stolen car speeded down the highway without any headlights.

Rewrite, beginning with

Although the stolen car didn't have any headlights,

The next words will be

    a. down the highway it

    b. nonetheless speeding down

    c. and it speeded down

    d. it speeded down

17. Without the right tools, Jess cannot fix her bike.

Rewrite, beginning with

Jess cannot fix her bike

The next words will be

    a. with the right
    b. unless she has the right
    c. if she has the right
    d. having the right

18. Boring through the first three chapters, the book becomes exciting in the fourth.

Rewrite, beginning with

The book becomes exciting

The next words will be

    a. after the first three
    b. until the fourth
    c. after the fourth
    d. before the fourth

19. Simon didn't smell any roses as he walked through the garden.

Rewrite, beginning with

Walking through the garden,

The next words will be

    a. no roses could be smelled
    b. but Simon didn't smell any roses
    c. but smelling no roses
    d. Simon didn't smell any roses.

20. Howard applied sunscreen because he has sensitive skin.

Rewrite, beginning with

Since he has sensitive skin,

The next words will be

    a. sunscreen

    b. Howard applied

    c. applying

    d. because Howard applied

Answer Key

Reading
1. B
The correct answer because that fact is stated directly in the
passage. The passage explains that Anne taught Helen to
hear by allowing her to feel the vibrations in her throat.

2. A
We can infer that Anne is a patient teacher because she
did not leave or lose her temper when Helen bit or hit her;
she just kept trying to teach Helen. Choice B is incorrect
because Anne taught Helen to read and talk. Choice C is
incorrect because Anne could hear. She was partially blind,
not deaf. Choice D is incorrect because it does not have to
do with patience.

3. B
The passage states that it was hard for anyone but Anne to
understand Helen when she spoke. Choice A is incorrect
because the passage does not mention Helen spoke a foreign
language. Choice C is incorrect because there is no mention
of how quiet or loud Helen's voice was. Choice D is incorrect
because we know from reading the passage that Helen did
learn to speak.

4. D
 This question tests the reader's summarization skills. The
other choices A, B, and C focus on portions of the second
paragraph that are too narrow and do not relate to the
specific portion of text in question. The complexity of the
sentence may mislead students into selecting one of these
answers, but rearranging or restating the sentence will lead
the reader to the correct answer. In addition, choice A makes
an assumption that may or may not be true about the intentions of the company, choice B focuses on one product
rather than the idea of the products, and choice C makes an
assumption about women that may or may not be true and
is not supported by the text.

5. C
The cumulus stage of a thunderstorm is the beginning of the

thunderstorm.

This is taken directly from the passage, "The first stage of a thunderstorm is the cumulus, or developing stage."

6. D
The passage lists four ways that air is heated. One way is, heat created by water vapor condensing into liquid.

7. A
The sequence of events can be taken from these sentences:

As the moisture carried by the [1] air currents rises, it rapidly cools into liquid drops of water, which appear as cumulus clouds. As the water vapor condenses into liquid, it [2] releases heat, which warms the air. This in turn causes the air to become less dense than the surrounding dry air and [3] rise farther.

8. B
The correct answer can be found in the fourth sentence of the first paragraph.

Option A is incorrect because repenting begins the day AFTER Mardi Gras. Option C is incorrect because you can celebrate Mardi Gras without being a member of a Krewe.

Option D is incorrect because exploration does not play any role in a modern Mardi Gras celebration.

9. A
The second sentence is the last paragraph states that Krewes are led by the Kings and Queens. Therefore, you must have to be part of a Krewe to be its King or its Queen.

Option B is incorrect because it never states in the passage that only people from France can be Kings and Queen of Mardi Gras. Option C is incorrect because the passage says nothing about having to speak French. Option D is incorrect because the passage does state that the Kings and Queens throw doubloons, which is fake money.

10. C
The first sentences of BOTH the 2nd and 3rd paragraphs mention that French explorers started this tradition in New Orleans.

Options A, B and D are incorrect because they are just names of cities or countries listed in the 2nd paragraph.

11. D
Clouds in space are made of different materials attracted by gravity. Clouds on Earth are made of water droplets or ice crystals.

Choice D is the best answer. Notice also that Choice D is the most specific.

12. C
The main idea is the first sentence of the passage; a cloud is a visible mass of droplets or frozen crystals floating in the atmosphere above the surface of the Earth or other planetary body.

The main idea is very often the first sentence of the paragraph.

13. C
This question asks about the process, and gives choices that can be confirmed or eliminated easily.

From the passage, "Dense, deep clouds reflect most light, so they appear white, at least from the top. Cloud droplets scatter light very efficiently, so the farther into a cloud light travels, the weaker it gets. This accounts for the gray or dark appearance at the base of large clouds."

We can eliminate choice A, since water droplets inside the cloud do not reflect light is false.

We can eliminate choice B, since, water droplets outside the cloud reflect light, it appears dark, is false.

Choice C is correct.

14. B
The general tone is informal.

15. B
The statement, " Fewer people have aquariums in their office than at home," cannot be inferred from this article.

16. C
The author does not provide evidence for this statement.

17. B
The following statement is an opinion, " Aquarium gravel improves the aesthetics of the aquarium."

18. D
This question tests the reader's summarization skills. The question is asking very generally about the message of the passage, and the title, "Ways Characters Communicate in Theater," is one indication of that. The other choices A, B, and C are all directly from the text, and therefore readers may be inclined to select one of them, but are too specific to encapsulate the entirety of the passage and its message.

19. B
The paragraph on soliloquies mentions "To be or not to be," and it is from the context of that paragraph that readers may understand that because "To be or not to be" is a soliloquy, Hamlet will be introspective, or thoughtful, while delivering it. It is true that actors deliver soliloquies alone, and may be "solitary" (choice A), but "thoughtful" (choice B) is more true to the overall idea of the paragraph. Readers may choose C because drama and theater can be used interchangeably and the passage mentions that soliloquies are unique to theater (and therefore drama), but this answer is not specific enough to the paragraph in question. Readers may pick up on the theme of life and death and Hamlet's true intentions and select that he is "hopeless" (choice D), but those themes are not discussed either by this paragraph or passage, as a close textual reading and analysis confirms.

20. C
This question tests the reader's grammatical skills. Choice B seems logical, but parenthesis are actually considered to be

a stronger break in a sentence than commas are, and along this line of thinking, actually disrupt the sentence more.

Choices A and D make comparisons between theater and film that are simply not made in the passage, and may or may not be true. This detail does clarify the statement that asides are most unique to theater by adding that it is not completely unique to theater, which may have been why the author didn't chose not to delete it and instead used parentheses to designate the detail's importance (choice C).

21. A
An example of a cold-blooded animal that hibernates underground during the winter is the snake.

Snakes, such as garter snakes and western rattlesnakes, hibernate underground in large groups during the winter.

The second sentence reinforces the first.

The second sentence reinforces the first with supporting details.

22. C
The dog barked and ran.

The dog barked and ran after the postman who was delivering mail.

The second sentence expands on the first.

The second sentence expands on the first sentence because it expresses in greater detail why the dog barked and ran and who it ran after.

24. D
Aphids, pest commonly found on roses, are destroying my rose bushes.

If I spray my rose bushes with insecticidal soap, I will kill the aphids.

The second sentence proposes a solution for the problem

mentioned in the first sentence.

25. C
Ms. Apple received and reviewed her students', who all scored on the 99th percentile, standardized test results.

She discovered that most of her students performed at the highest level of achievement; thus, they have mastered the material and skills taught.

The second sentence analyzes a statement made in the first (a part of the first sentence).

26. C
Human activities have contributed to global warming.

Due to global warming, hurricanes, tornadoes and other storms will become stronger and more frequent.

The second sentence states an effect of global warming.

27. D
Jungles and rainforests are both associated with tropical climates.

Vegetation in jungles are tangled and impenetrable (hard to walk through without cutting your way through); however, vegetation in the rainforest is sparse.

The second sentence describes the differences between jungles and rainforests whereas the first compares their similarities.

28. B
Rosaline's friend invited her to the Civil Rights Photography Exhibit at the local museum.

Rosaline did not know as much as she wanted to about the African-American Civil Rights Movement, so she went to the library and checked out books related to the African-American Civil Rights Movement.

The second sentence provides a problem and solution.

29. A
Parrots and macaws are beautiful, colorful birds.

There are over 370 species of parrots, but there are only 18 species of macaws.

The second sentence describes the differences between parrots and macaws whereas the first compares their similarities.

30. B
Paris is often called the "City of Lights."

Paris is called the "City of Lights" because there are over 296 illuminated sites and buildings in Paris, and most importantly, Paris was the birthplace of the Age of Enlightenment.

The second sentence reinforces the first sentences claim with supporting details.

Arithmetic

1. C
If there are 5 friends and each drink costs $1.89, we can round up to $2 per drink and estimate the total cost at, 5 X $2 = $10.
The actual, cost is 5 X $1.89 = $9.45.

2. A
$2cnx = 2(4 \times 5 \times 3) =, 2 \times 60/2 \times 5 =, 120/10 = 12$

3. D
$75/1500 = 15/300 = 3/60 = 1/20$

4. C
16 X 230 is about 3,100. The actual number is 3680.

5. B

Day	Number of Absent Students	Number of Present Students	% Attendance

Monday	5	40	88.88%
Tuesday	9	36	80.00%
Wednesday	4	41	91.11%
Thursday	10	35	77.77%
Friday	6	39	86.66%

To find the average or mean, sum the series and divide by the number of items.
88.88 + 80.00 + 91.11 + 77.77 + 86.66/5
424.42/5 = 84.88
Round up to 85%.

Percentage attendance will be 85%

6. C
Let the original price be 100x.

At the rate of 7% discount, the discount will be 100x•7/100 = 7x. So, the discounted price will be = 100x - 7x = 93x.

Over this price, at the rate of 2% additional discount, the discount will be 93x•2/100 = 1.86x. So, the additionally discounted price will be = 93x - 1.86x = 91.14x.

This is the amount which John has paid for the jacket:

91.14x = 425

x = 425 / 91.14 = 4.6631

The jacket costs 100x. So, 100x = 100•4.6631 = $466.31.

When rounded to the nearest whole number, this is equal to $466.

7. B
215 X 65 is about 13,500. The exact answer is 13,975.

8. C
10 x 2 – (7 + 9) = 4. This is an order of operations question. Do the brackets first, then multiplication and division, then addition and subtraction.

9. B
40/100 X = 90
40X = (90 * 100) = 9000
x = 9000/40 = 900/4 = 225
Half of 225 = 112.5

10. B
First, see if you can eliminate any options. 1/4 + 1/3 is going to equal about 1/2.

Option A, 9/10 is very close to 1, so it can be eliminated. Options B and C are very close to 1/2 so they should be considered. Option D is less than half and very close to zero, so it can be eliminated.

Looking at the denominators, option C has denominator of 15, and option B has denominator of 20. Right away, notice that 20 is common multiple of 4 and 10, and 15 is not.

11. C
1 inch on map = 2,000 inches on ground. So, 5.2 inches on map = 5.2•2,000 = 10,400 inches on ground.

12. B
Actual cost = X, therefore, 545 = x + 0.15x, 545 = 1x + 0.15x, 545 = 1.15x, x = 545/1.15 = 473.9

13. C
0.27 + 0.33 = 0.60 and 0.60 = 60/100 = 3/5

14. D
First, we need to convert all units to grams. Since 1000 g = 1 kg:

10 kg 550 g = 10•1000 g + 550 g = 10,000 g + 550 g = 10,550 g.

10,550 g is shared between 5 men. So each man will have to carry 10,550/5 = 2,110 g

2,110 g = 2,000 g + 110 g = 2 kg 110 g

15. D
A common denominator is needed, a number which both 4

and 16 will divide into. So, 4+11/16 = 15/16

16. B
As the lawn is square , the length of one side will be the square root of the area. √62,500 = 250 meters. So, the perimeter is found by 4 times the length of the side of the square:

250•4 = 1000 meters.

Since each meter costs $5.5, the total cost of the fence will be 1000•5.5 = $5,500.

17. A
The easiest way to solve age problems is to use a table:

	Mother	Child
Now	7x	x
25 years later	7x + 25	x + 25

Now, mother is 7 times older than her child. So, if we say that the child is x years old, mother is 7x years old. In 25 years, 25 will be added to their ages. We are told that in 25 years, mother's age will double her child's age. So,

7x + 25 = 2(x + 25) ... by solving this equation, we reach x that is the child's age:

7x + 25 = 2x + 50

7x - 2x = 50 - 25

5x = 25

x = 5

Mother is 7x years old: 7x = 7•5 = 35

18. A
0.28 = 28/100 = 7/25

19. C
By the given information in the question, we understand that the discounted part is the saved amount. If we say that the original price of the desk is 100x; by 20% discount rate,

20x will be the discounted part:

20x = 45

We know that Mark paid 20% less than the original price. So, he paid 100x - 20x = 80x. We are asked to find 80x. With a simple direct proportion, we can find the result:

20x = 45

80x = ?

By cross multiplication, we find the result:

? = 80x•45 / 20x = 4•45 = $180

20. C
Let the number be x.

x/(3/2) is the required result.

x•(3/2) is the operation the student does mistakenly. We are told that the multiplication result is 5 more than the division result that is the required one:

x•(3/2) = x/(3/2) + 5 ... by solving this equation, we find x.

3x/2 = 2x/3 + 5

3x/2 - 2x/3 = 5 ... by equating the denominators to 6:

9x/6 - 4x/6 = 5

(9x - 4x)/6 = 5

5x/6 = 5

5x = 30

x = 6

Algebra

21. C
243/(3 x 3 x 3) = 243/27 = 9

22. B
4y + 24 = 3y + 30, = 4y – 3y + 24 = 30, = y + 24 = 30, = y =
30 – 24, = y = 6

23. B
$(x^2 - y^2) / (x - y) = x + y$

$$\frac{-(x^2 - xy)}{xy - y^2}$$

$$\frac{-(xy - y^2)}{0}$$

24. A
10 x 10 x 100 x 100 = 1000^x, =100 x 10,000 = 1000^x, =
1,000,000 = 1000^x = x = 2

25. C
We are asked to find A + B - C. By paying attention to the
sign distribution; we write the polynomials and operate:

$A + B \quad C - (2x^4 + x^2 \quad 3x) + (x^4 - x^3 + 5) - (x^4 + 2x^3 + 4x + 5)$

$= -2x^4 + x^2 - 3x + x^4 - x^3 + 5 - x^4 - 2x^3 - 4x - 5$

$= -2x^4 + x^4 - x^4 - x^3 - 2x^3 + x^2 - 3x - 4x + 5 - 5$ ... similar terms
written together to ease summing/substituting.

$= -2x^4 - 3x^3 + x^2 - 7x$

26. C
To find the solution for the inequality, we need to simplify it
first:

$(x - 6)^2 \geq x^2 + 12$ ... we can write the open form of the left
side:

$x^2 - 12x + 36 \geq x^2 + 12$ ... x^2 terms on both sides cancel each
other:

$-12x + 36 \geq 12$ ... Now, we aim to have x alone on one side.

So, we subtract 36 from both sides:

-12x + 36 - 36 ≥ 12 - 36

-12x ≥ -24 ... We divide both sides by -12. This means that the inequality will change its direction:

x ≤ 2 ... x can be 2 or a smaller value.

This result is shown by (-∞, 2].

27. B
(7 x 7 x 7 x 7 x 7) - (3 x 3 x 3 x 3 x 3) = 16,807 – 243 = 16,564.

28. C
$(x^3 - 3x^2 + 3x - 1) / (x - 1) = x^2 - 2x + 1$
$\underline{-(x^3 - x^2)}$
   $-2x^2 + 3x - 1$
$\underline{-(-2 x^2 + 2x)}$
        $x - 1$

$\underline{-(x - 1)}$
0

29. C
Exponential form is 9^3 and standard from is 729

30. B
$x^2 - 5x - 6 = 0$

We try to separate the middle term -5x to find common factors with x^2 and -6 separately:

$x^2 - 6x + x - 6 = 0$ ... Here, we see that x is a common factor for x^2 and -6x:

x(x - 6) + x - 6 = 0 ... Here, we have x times x - 6 and 1 time x - 6 summed up. This means that we have x + 1 times x - 6:

(x + 1)(x - 6) = 0 ... This is true when either or both of the expressions in the parenthesis are equal to zero:

x + 1 = 0 ... x = -1

x - 6 = 0 ... x = 6

-1 and 6 are the solutions for this quadratic equation.

31. B
0.524/ (10•10•10) = 0.524/1000 ... This means that we need to carry the decimal point 3 decimals left from the point it is now:

= 0.0.0.0.524 = 0.000524

The correct answer is (b).

32. A
We need to find the greatest common divisor of the two terms in order to factor the expression. We should remember that if the bases of exponent numbers are the same, the multiplication of two terms is found by summing the powers and writing on the same base. Similarly; when dividing, the power of the divisor is subtracted from the power of the divided.

Both x^3y^3 and x^2y^8 contain x^2 and y^3. So;

$x^3y^3 - x^2y^8 = x•x^2y^3 - y^5•x^2y^3$ ... We can carry x^2y^3 out as the factor:

$= x^2y^3(x - y^5)$

33. D
Our aim to collect the knowns on one side and the unknowns (x terms) on the other side:

$5x/2 = (3x + 24)/6$ ... First, we can simplify the denominators of both sides by 2:

$5x = (3x + 24)/3$ ... Now, we can do cross multiplication:

$15x = 3x + 24$

$15x - 3x = 24$

$12x = 24$

$x = 24/12 = 2$

34. D
When multiplying exponents with the same base, add the

exponents. $3^2 \times 3^5 = 3^{2+5} = 3^7$

35. C
Solving the system means finding x and y. Since we also have a in the system, we will find x and y depending on a.

We can obtain y by using the equation ax + y = 1:

y = 1 - ax ... Then, we can insert this value into the second equation:

x + a(1 - ax) = 1

$x + a - a^2x = 1$

$x - a^2x = 1 - a$

$x(1 - a^2) = 1 - a$ ... We need to obtain x alone:

$x = (1 - a)/(1 - a^2)$ ... Here, $1 - a^2 = (1 - a)(1 + a)$ is used:

x = (1 - a)/((1 - a)(1 + a)) ... Simplifying by (1 - a):

x = 1/(a + 1) ... Now we know the value of x. By using either of the equations, we can find the value of y. Let us use y = 1 - ax:

y = 1 - a•1/(a + 1)

y = 1 - a/(a + 1) ... By writing on the same denominator:

y = ((a + 1) - a)/(a + 1)

y = (a + 1 - a)/(a + 1) ... a and -a cancel each other:

y = 1/(a + 1) ... x and y are found to be equal.

The solution of the system is (1/(a + 1), 1/(a + 1))

36. A
To divide exponents with the same base, subtract the exponents. $3^{8-5} = 3^3$

37. C
To solve the linear equation, we operate the knowns and unknowns within each other and try to obtain x term (which is the unknown) alone on one side of the equation:

3(x + 2) - 2(1 - x) = 4x + 5 ... We remove the parenthesis by distributing the factors:

$3x + 6 - 2 + 2x = 4x + 5$

$5x + 4 = 4x + 5$

$5x - 4x = 5 - 4$

$x = 1$

38. C
$3x^a + 6a^x - x^a + (-5a^x) - 2x^a = 3x^a + 6a^x - x^a - 5a^x - 2x^a = a^x$

39. B
By paying attention to the sign distribution; we write the polynomials and operate:
$(-3x^2 + 2x + 6) + (-x^2 - x - 1)$

$= -3x^2 + 2x + 6 - x^2 - x - 1$

$= -3x^2 - x^2 + 2x - x + 6 - 1$ ... similar terms written together to ease summing/substituting.

$= -4x^2 + x + 5$

40. A
10^4 is not equal to $100,000$
$10^4 = 10 \times 10 \times 10 \times 10 = 10^2 \times 10^2 = 10,000$

College Level

41. D
Comparing angles on similar triangles, a, b and c will be $70°$, $35°$, $35°$

42. D
$\log_x 125 = 3$ ... we use the property that $\log_a a^b = b \cdot \log_a a = b$

$\log_x 125 = 3 \cdot \log_x x$

$\log_x 125 = \log_x x^3$ ... We can cancel the $\log_x$ function on both sides:

$125 = x^3$

$5^3 = x^3$

$5 = x$

So; x = 5

43. C

$(1 - 4\sin^2(\pi/6))/(1+4\cos^2(\pi/3)) = (1 - 4\sin^2(30°))/(1 + 4\cos^2(60°))$

We know that sin30° = cos60° = 1/2

$(1 - 4\sin^2(30°))/(1 + 4\cos^2(60°)) = (1 - 4•(1/2)^2)/(1 + 4•(1/2)^2)$

$= (1 - 4•(1/4))/(1 + 4•(1/4))$

$= (1 - 1)/(1 + 1) = 0/2 = 0$

44. A

We know that sin30° = cos60° = 1/2, sin0° = cos90° = 0

$(\sin^2 30° - \sin0°)/(\cos90° - \cos60°) = ((1/2)^2 - 0)/(0 - (1/2))$

$= (1/4)/(-1/2) = -1/2$

45. A

Yes the triangles are congruent.

46. D

Perimeter of triangle ABC is asked.
Perimeter of a triangle = sum of all three sides.

Here, Perimeter of ΔABC = |AC| + |CB| + |AB|.

Since the triangle is located in the middle of two adjacent and identical rectangles, we find the side lengths using these rectangles:

|AB| = 6 + 6 = 12 cm

|CB| = 8.5 cm

|AC| = |CB| = 8.5 cm

Perimeter = |AC| + |CB| + |AB| = 8.5 + 8.5 + 12 = 29 cm

47. B

$a = 90°$

$\cot 90° = \cos 90° / \sin 90° = 0/1 = 0$

48. A

First, we need to simplify the value of angle a:

$a = 3\pi/2 - \pi/6 - \pi - \pi/3$ ... by equating the denominators at 6:

$a = 9\pi/6 - \pi/6 - 6\pi/6 - 2\pi/6$

$a = (9 - 1 - 6 - 2)\pi/6$

$a = 0 \cdot \pi /6$

$a = 0$

$\sin a = \sin 0° = 0$

49. A

$\log_x(9/25) = 2$ ... we use the property that $\log_a a^b = b \cdot \log_a a = b$

$\log_x(9/25) = 2 \cdot \log_x x$

$\log_x(9/25) = \log_x x^2$ ... We can cancel the $\log_x$ function on both sides:

$9/25 = x^2$

$(3/5)^2 = x^2$ ... We can remove the power 2 in both sides:

$3/5 = x$

So; $x = 3/5$

50. A

We are given that,

$a_0 = 1/2$

$a_n = 2a_{n-1}^2$

Starting from the zeroth term, we can reach the second term:

$n = 1$ ... $a_1 = 2a_0^2 = 2(1/2)^2 = 2(1/4) = 1/2$

$n = 2$ ... $a_2 = 2a_1^2 = 2(1/2)^2 = 2(1/4) = 1/2$

51. A

The wheel travels $2\pi r$ distance when it makes one revolution. Here, r stands for the radius. The radius is given as 25 cm in the figure. So,
$2\pi r = 2\pi \cdot 25 = 50\pi$ cm is the distance travelled in one revolution.

In 175 revolutions: $175 \cdot 50\pi = 8750\pi$ cm is travelled.

We are asked to find the distance in meter.

1 m = 100 cm So;

8750π cm $= 8750\pi / 100 = 87.5\pi$ m

52. D

We are given that,

$a_n = (-1)^n a_{n-1}$

$a_2 = 2$

Starting from the second term, we can reach the zeroth term in the reverse direction:

$n = 2 \ldots a_2 = (-1)^2 a_1 \ldots 2 = a_1$

$n = 1 \ldots a_1 = (-1)^1 a_0 \ldots 2 = -a_0 \ldots a_0 = -2$

53. A

If a line represents an equation, all points on that line should satisfy the equation. Meaning that all (x, y) pairs present on the line should be able to verify that 2y - x is equal to 4. We can find out the correct line by trying a (x, y) point existing on each line. It is easier to choose points on the intersection of the gridlines:

Let us try the point (4, 4) on line A:

$2 \cdot 4 - 4 = 4$

$8 - 4 = 4$

$4 = 4 \ldots$ this is a correct result, so the equation for line A is $2y - x = 4$.

Let us try other points to check the other lines:

Point (-1, 2) on line B:

2•2 - (-1) = 4

4 + 1 = 4

5 = 4 ... this is a wrong result, so the equation for line B is not 2y - x = 4.

Point (3, -1) on line C:

2•(-1) - 3 = 4

-2 - 3 = 4

-5 = 4 ... this is a wrong result, so the equation for line C is not 2y - x = 4.

Point (-2, -1) on line D:

2•(-1) - (-2) = 4

-2 + 2 = 4

0 = 4 ... this is a wrong result, so the equation for line D is not 2y - x = 4.

54. D
We know that;

tgα = sinα/cosα

ctgα = cosα/sinα

So;

tgα/ctgα = (sinα/cosα)•(cosα/sinα) = (sinα • cosα)/(sinα • cosα)

sinα terms and cosα terms cancel each other in the nominator and the denominator:

tgα/ctgα = 1

55. D
To understand this question better, let us draw a right triangle by writing the given data on it:

The side opposite to angle α is named by a.

cos α = length of the adjacent side / length of the hypotenuse = b/c

cos α = 3/5 is given. This means that b/c = 3/5

b = 24 is also given:

24/c = 3/5 ... By cross multiplication:

24•5 = 3c ... Simplifying both sides by 3:

8•5 = c

c = 40

56. C
In a right angle, Pythagorean Theorem is applicable:
$a^2 + b^2 = c^2$ ... Here, a and b represent the adjacent and opposite sides, c represents the hypotenuse. Hypotenuse is larger than the other two sides.

In this question, we need to try each answer choice by applying $a^2 + b^2 = c^2$ to see if it is satisfied; by inserting the largest number into c:

a. 1, 2, 3:

$1^2 + 2^2 = 3^2$

$1 + 4 = 9$

5 = 9 ... This is not correct, so answer choice does not represent a right angle whose sides are consecutive numbers.

b. 2, 3, 4:

$2^2 + 3^2 = 4^2$

$4 + 9 = 16$

13 = 16 ... This is not correct, so this answer choice does

not represent a right angle whose sides are consecutive numbers.

c. 3, 4, 5:

$3^2 + 4^2 = 5^2$

$9 + 16 = 25$

25 = 25 ... This is correct, 3, 4, 5 are also consecutive numbers; so this answer choice represents a right angle whose sides are consecutive numbers.

d. 4, 5, 6:

$4^2 + 5^2 = 6^2$

$16 + 25 = 36$

41 = 36 ... This is not correct, so this answer choice does not represent a right angle whose sides are consecutive numbers.

57. A
If we call one side of the square "a," the area of the square will be a^2.

We know that $a^2 = 200$ cm^2.

On the other hand; there is an isosceles right triangle. Using the **Pythagorean Theorem**:

(Hypotenuse)^2 = (Perpendicular)^2 + (Base)^2
$h^2 = a^2 + b^2$

Given: $h^2 = 200$, a = b = x
Then, $x^2 + x^2 = 200$, $2x^2 = 200$, $x^2 = 100$
x = 10

58. C
We know that $\pi/2 = 90°$

$\cos 90° = 0$, $\sin 90° = 1$

$ctg 90° = \cos 90° / \sin 90° = 0/1 = 0$ So;

$(\cos(\pi/2) + \text{ctg}(\pi/2))/\sin(\pi/2) = (\cos 90° + \text{ctg} 90°)/\sin 90° = (0 + 0)/1 = 0$

59. B

In the question, we have a right triangle formed inside the circle. We are asked to find the length of the hypotenuse of this triangle. We can find the other two sides of the triangle by using circle properties:

The diameter of the circle is equal to 12 cm. The legs of the right triangle are the radii of the circle; so they are 6 cm long.

Using the **Pythagorean Theorem:**

$(\text{Hypotenuse})^2 = (\text{Perpendicular})^2 + (\text{Base})^2$
$h^2 = a^2 + b^2$

Given: d (diameter)= 12 & r (radius) = a = b = 6
$h^2 = a^2 + b^2$
$h^2 = 6^2 + 6^2,\ h^2 = 36 + 36$
$h^2 = 72$
$h = \sqrt{72}$
$h = 8.48$

60. C

Slope (m) = $\dfrac{\text{change in y}}{\text{change in x}}$

$(x_1, y_1)=(-3,1)$ & $(x_2, y_2)= (1,-4)$
Slope = $[-4 - 1]/[1-(-3)]= -5/4$

Sentence Skills

1. A

The third conditional is used for talking about an unreal situation (that did not happen) in the past. For example, "If I had studied harder, [if clause] I would have passed the exam [main clause]. Which is the same as, "I failed the exam, because I didn't study hard enough."

2. C
Double negative sentence. In double negative sentences, one of the negatives is replaced with "any."

3. B
The sentence refers to a person, so "who" is the only correct option.

4. A
The sentence requires the past perfect "has always been known." Furthermore, this is the only grammatically correct choice.

5. B
The superlative, "hottest," is used when expressing a temperature greater than that of anything to which it is being compared.

6. C
When comparing two items, use "the taller." When comparing more than two items, use "the tallest."

7. B
The past perfect form is used to describe an event that occurred in the past and prior to another event.

8. A
The subject is "rules" so the present tense plural form, "are," is used to agree with "realize."

9. C
The simple past tense, "had," is correct because it refers to completed action in the past.

10. C
The simple past tense, "sank," is correct because it refers to completed action in the past.

11. A
The order must be: second act, and then intermission. "Came after" is the only synonym of "followed."

12. D
Thomas discovered not gradually, but suddenly: hence "when" instead of "as."

13. B
"To protect their puppy from wild coyotes" combines "because of the wild coyotes" and   "for their puppy" while preserving the original meaning.

14. B
"As you invest more" retains the parallel structure grammatically.

15. C
"Necessary" must modify "owning"; "while" already replaces "but."

16. D
The main clause must start with the main subject, "it." No conjunction is needed in addition to "although."

17. B
The only phrase that preserves the use of "without" is "unless."

18. A
The correct sequence is, boring for the first three chapters, then exciting. So, the book is not exciting until after the first three chapters.

19. D
The main clause must begin with "Simon," the main subject, which is modified by "walking."

20. B
"Since" replaces "because" as the subordinating conjunction. The main clause must begin with "Howard."

Practice Test Questions Set 2

T he questions below are not the same as you will find on the Accuplacer® - that would be too easy! And nobody knows what the questions will be and they change all the time. Below are general questions that cover the same subject areas as the Accuplacer®. So, while the format and exact wording of the questions may differ slightly, and change from year to year, if you can answer the questions below, you will have no problem with the Accuplacer®.

For the best results, take these Practice Test Questions as if it were the real exam. Set aside time when you will not be disturbed, and a location that is quiet and free of distractions. Read the instructions carefully, read each question carefully, and answer to the best of your ability.
Use the bubble answer sheets provided. When you have completed the Practice Questions, check your answer against the Answer Key and read the explanation provided.

Do not attempt more than one set of practice test questions in one day. After completing the first practice test, wait two or three days before attempting the second set of questions.

Reading Answer Sheet

1. Ⓐ Ⓑ Ⓒ Ⓓ   11. Ⓐ Ⓑ Ⓒ Ⓓ   21. Ⓐ Ⓑ Ⓒ Ⓓ

2. Ⓐ Ⓑ Ⓒ Ⓓ   12. Ⓐ Ⓑ Ⓒ Ⓓ   22. Ⓐ Ⓑ Ⓒ Ⓓ

3. Ⓐ Ⓑ Ⓒ Ⓓ   13. Ⓐ Ⓑ Ⓒ Ⓓ   23. Ⓐ Ⓑ Ⓒ Ⓓ

4. Ⓐ Ⓑ Ⓒ Ⓓ   14. Ⓐ Ⓑ Ⓒ Ⓓ   24. Ⓐ Ⓑ Ⓒ Ⓓ

5. Ⓐ Ⓑ Ⓒ Ⓓ   15. Ⓐ Ⓑ Ⓒ Ⓓ   25. Ⓐ Ⓑ Ⓒ Ⓓ

6. Ⓐ Ⓑ Ⓒ Ⓓ   16. Ⓐ Ⓑ Ⓒ Ⓓ   26. Ⓐ Ⓑ Ⓒ Ⓓ

7. Ⓐ Ⓑ Ⓒ Ⓓ   17. Ⓐ Ⓑ Ⓒ Ⓓ   27. Ⓐ Ⓑ Ⓒ Ⓓ

8. Ⓐ Ⓑ Ⓒ Ⓓ   18. Ⓐ Ⓑ Ⓒ Ⓓ   28. Ⓐ Ⓑ Ⓒ Ⓓ

9. Ⓐ Ⓑ Ⓒ Ⓓ   19. Ⓐ Ⓑ Ⓒ Ⓓ   29. Ⓐ Ⓑ Ⓒ Ⓓ

10. Ⓐ Ⓑ Ⓒ Ⓓ   20. Ⓐ Ⓑ Ⓒ Ⓓ   30. Ⓐ Ⓑ Ⓒ Ⓓ

Mathematics Answer Sheet
(Arithmetic, Algebra and College Level Math)

1. Ⓐ Ⓑ Ⓒ Ⓓ   21. Ⓐ Ⓑ Ⓒ Ⓓ   41. Ⓐ Ⓑ Ⓒ Ⓓ

2. Ⓐ Ⓑ Ⓒ Ⓓ   22. Ⓐ Ⓑ Ⓒ Ⓓ   42. Ⓐ Ⓑ Ⓒ Ⓓ

3. Ⓐ Ⓑ Ⓒ Ⓓ   23. Ⓐ Ⓑ Ⓒ Ⓓ   43. Ⓐ Ⓑ Ⓒ Ⓓ

4. Ⓐ Ⓑ Ⓒ Ⓓ   24. Ⓐ Ⓑ Ⓒ Ⓓ   44. Ⓐ Ⓑ Ⓒ Ⓓ

5. Ⓐ Ⓑ Ⓒ Ⓓ   25. Ⓐ Ⓑ Ⓒ Ⓓ   45. Ⓐ Ⓑ Ⓒ Ⓓ

6. Ⓐ Ⓑ Ⓒ Ⓓ   26. Ⓐ Ⓑ Ⓒ Ⓓ   46. Ⓐ Ⓑ Ⓒ Ⓓ

7. Ⓐ Ⓑ Ⓒ Ⓓ   27. Ⓐ Ⓑ Ⓒ Ⓓ   47. Ⓐ Ⓑ Ⓒ Ⓓ

8. Ⓐ Ⓑ Ⓒ Ⓓ   28. Ⓐ Ⓑ Ⓒ Ⓓ   48. Ⓐ Ⓑ Ⓒ Ⓓ

9. Ⓐ Ⓑ Ⓒ Ⓓ   29. Ⓐ Ⓑ Ⓒ Ⓓ   49. Ⓐ Ⓑ Ⓒ Ⓓ

10. Ⓐ Ⓑ Ⓒ Ⓓ   30. Ⓐ Ⓑ Ⓒ Ⓓ   50. Ⓐ Ⓑ Ⓒ Ⓓ

11. Ⓐ Ⓑ Ⓒ Ⓓ   31. Ⓐ Ⓑ Ⓒ Ⓓ   51. Ⓐ Ⓑ Ⓒ Ⓓ

12. Ⓐ Ⓑ Ⓒ Ⓓ   32. Ⓐ Ⓑ Ⓒ Ⓓ   52. Ⓐ Ⓑ Ⓒ Ⓓ

13. Ⓐ Ⓑ Ⓒ Ⓓ   33. Ⓐ Ⓑ Ⓒ Ⓓ   53. Ⓐ Ⓑ Ⓒ Ⓓ

14. Ⓐ Ⓑ Ⓒ Ⓓ   34. Ⓐ Ⓑ Ⓒ Ⓓ   54. Ⓐ Ⓑ Ⓒ Ⓓ

15. Ⓐ Ⓑ Ⓒ Ⓓ   35. Ⓐ Ⓑ Ⓒ Ⓓ   55. Ⓐ Ⓑ Ⓒ Ⓓ

16. Ⓐ Ⓑ Ⓒ Ⓓ   36. Ⓐ Ⓑ Ⓒ Ⓓ   56. Ⓐ Ⓑ Ⓒ Ⓓ

17. Ⓐ Ⓑ Ⓒ Ⓓ   37. Ⓐ Ⓑ Ⓒ Ⓓ   57. Ⓐ Ⓑ Ⓒ Ⓓ

18. Ⓐ Ⓑ Ⓒ Ⓓ   38. Ⓐ Ⓑ Ⓒ Ⓓ   58. Ⓐ Ⓑ Ⓒ Ⓓ

19. Ⓐ Ⓑ Ⓒ Ⓓ   39. Ⓐ Ⓑ Ⓒ Ⓓ   59. Ⓐ Ⓑ Ⓒ Ⓓ

20. Ⓐ Ⓑ Ⓒ Ⓓ   40. Ⓐ Ⓑ Ⓒ Ⓓ   60. Ⓐ Ⓑ Ⓒ Ⓓ

Sentence Skills Answer Sheet

1. (A) (B) (C) (D)   11. (A) (B) (C) (D)

2. (A) (B) (C) (D)   12. (A) (B) (C) (D)

3. (A) (B) (C) (D)   13. (A) (B) (C) (D)

4. (A) (B) (C) (D)   14. (A) (B) (C) (D)

5. (A) (B) (C) (D)   15. (A) (B) (C) (D)

6. (A) (B) (C) (D)   16. (A) (B) (C) (D)

7. (A) (B) (C) (D)   17. (A) (B) (C) (D)

8. (A) (B) (C) (D)   18. (A) (B) (C) (D)

9. (A) (B) (C) (D)   19. (A) (B) (C) (D)

10. (A) (B) (C) (D)   20. (A) (B) (C) (D)

Part 1 – Reading and Language Arts

Questions 1 - 4 refer to the following passage.

The Civil War

The Civil War began on April 12, 1861. The first shots of the Civil War were fired in Fort Sumter, South Carolina. Note that even though more American lives were lost in the Civil War than in any other war, not one person died on that first day. The war began because eleven Southern states seceded from the Union and tried to start their own government, The Confederate States of America.

Why did the states secede? The issue of slavery was a primary cause of the Civil War. The eleven southern states relied heavily on their slaves to foster their farming and plantation lifestyles. The northern states, many of whom had already abolished slavery, did not feel that the southern states should have slaves. The north wanted to free all the slaves and President Lincoln's goal was to both end slavery and preserve the Union. He had Congress declare war on the Confederacy on April 14, 1862. For four long, blood soaked years, the North and South fought.

From 1861 to mid 1863, it seemed as if the South would win this war. However, on July 1, 1863, an epic three day battle was waged on a field in Gettysburg, Pennsylvania. Gettysburg is remembered for being one of the bloodiest battles in American history. At the end of the three days, the North turned the tide of the war in their favor. The North then went on to dominate the South for the remainder of the war. Most well remembered might be General Sherman's "March to The Sea," where he famously led the Union Army through Georgia and the Carolinas, burning and destroying everything in their path.

In 1865, the Union army invaded and captured the Confederate capital of Richmond Virginia. Robert E. Lee, leader of the Confederacy surrendered to General Ulysses S. Grant,

leader of the Union forces, on April 9, 1865. The Civil War
was over and the Union was preserved.

1. What does secede mean?

    a. To break away from

    b. To accomplish

    c. To join

    d. To lose

2. Which of the following statements summarizes a FACT from the passage?

    a. Congress declared war and then the Battle of Fort Sumter began.

    b. Congress declared war after shots were fired at Fort Sumter.

    c. President Lincoln was pro slavery

    d. President Lincoln was at Fort Sumter with Congress

3. Which event finally led the Confederacy to surrender?

    a. The battle of Gettysburg

    b. The battle of Bull Run

    c. The invasion of the confederate capital of Richmond

    d. Sherman's March to the Sea

4. The word abolish as used in this passage most nearly means?

    a. To ban

    b. To polish

    c. To support

    d. To destroy

Questions 5 - 8 refer to the following passage.

Lightning

Lightning is an electrical discharge that occurs in a thunderstorm. Often you'll see it as a bright "bolt" (or streak) coming from the sky. Lightning occurs when static electricity inside clouds builds up and causes an electrical charge. What causes the static electricity? Water! Specifically, water droplets collide with ice crystals after the temperature in the cloud falls below freezing. Sometimes these collisions are small, but other times they're quite large. Large collisions cause large electrical charges, and when they're large enough, look out! The hyper-charged cloud will emit a burst of lightning. This lightning looks quite impressive. For a good reason, too: A lightning bolt's temperature gets so hot that it's sometimes five times hotter than the sun's surface. Although the lightning bolt is hot, it's also short-lived. Because of that, when a person is unfortunate enough to be struck by lightning, their odds of surviving are pretty good. Statistics show that 90% of victims survive a lightning blast. Oh, and that old saying, "Lightning never strikes twice in the same spot?" It's a myth! Many people report surviving lightning blasts three or more times. What's more, lightning strikes some skyscrapers multiple times. The other prominent feature of lightning storms is the thunder. This is caused by the super-heated air around a lightning bolt expands at the speed of sound. We hear thunder after seeing the lightning bolt because sound travels slower than the speed of light. In reality, though, both occur at the same moment. [3]

5. What can we infer from this passage?

a. An electrical discharge in the clouds causes lightning.

b. Lightning is not as hot as the temperature of the sun's surface.

c. The sound that lightning makes occurs when electricity strikes an object.

d. We hear lightning before we see it.

6. Being struck by lightning means:

   a. Instant death.

   b. Less than a fifty percent chance of survival.

   c. A ninety percent chance of surviving the strike.

   d. An eighty percent chance of survival.

7. Lightning is caused by the following:

   a. Water droplets colliding with ice crystals creating static electricity.

   b. Friction from the clouds rubbing together.

   c. Water droplets colliding.

   d. Warm and cold air mixing together.

Questions 9 - 12 refer to the following passage.

Low Blood Sugar

As the name suggest, low blood sugar is low sugar levels in the bloodstream. This can occur when you have not eaten properly and undertake strenuous activity, or, when you are very hungry. When Low blood sugar occurs regularly and is ongoing, it is a medical condition called hypoglycemia. This condition can occur in diabetics and in healthy adults.

Causes of low blood sugar can include excessive alcohol consumption, metabolic problems, stomach surgery, pancreas, liver or kidneys problems, as well as a side-effect of some medications.

Symptoms

There are different symptoms depending on the severity of the case.

Mild hypoglycemia can lead to feelings of nausea and hunger. The patient may also feel nervous, jittery and have fast heart beats. Sweaty skin, clammy and cold skin are likely symptoms.

Moderate hypoglycemia can result in a short temper, confusion, nervousness, fear and blurring of vision. The patient may feel weak and unsteady.

Severe cases of hypoglycemia can lead to seizures, coma, fainting spells, nightmares, headaches, excessive sweats and severe tiredness.

Diagnosis of low blood sugar

A doctor can diagnosis this medical condition by asking the patient questions and testing blood and urine samples. Home testing kits are available for patients to monitor blood sugar levels. It is important to see a qualified doctor though. The doctor can administer tests to ensure that will safely rule out other medical conditions that could affect blood sugar levels.

Treatment

Quick treatments include drinking or eating foods and drinks with high sugar contents. Good examples include soda, fruit juice, hard candy and raisins. Glucose energy tablets can also help. Doctors may also recommend medications and well as changes in diet and exercise routine to treat chronic low blood sugar.

9. Based on the article, which of the following is true?

    a. Low blood sugar can happen to anyone.

    b. Low blood sugar only happens to diabetics.

    c. Low blood sugar can occur even.

    d. None of the statements are true.

10. Which of the following are the author's opinion?

    a. Quick treatments include drinking or eating foods and drinks with high sugar contents.

    b. None of the statements are opinions.

    c. This condition can occur in diabetics and also in healthy adults.

    d. There are different symptoms depending on the severity of the case

11. What is the author's purpose?

    a. To inform

    b. To persuade

    c. To entertain

    d. To analyze

12. Which of the following is not a detail?

    a. A doctor can diagnosis this medical condition by asking the patient questions and testing.

    b. A doctor will test blood and urine samples.

    c. Glucose energy tablets can also help.

    d. Home test kits monitor blood sugar levels.

Questions 13 - 16 refer to the following passage.

Myths, Legend and Folklore

Cultural historians draw a distinction between myth, legend and folktale simply as a way to group traditional stories. However, in many cultures, drawing a sharp line between myths and legends is not that simple. Instead of dividing their traditional stories into myths, legends, and folktales, some cultures divide them into two categories. The first category roughly corresponds to folktales, and the second is one that combines myths and legends. Similarly, we can not always separate myths from folktales. One society might consider a story true, making it a myth. Another society may believe the story is fiction, which makes it a folktale. In fact, when a myth loses its status as part of a religious system, it often takes on traits more typical of folktales, with its formerly divine characters now appearing as human heroes, giants, or fairies. Myth, legend, and folktale are only a few of the categories of traditional stories. Other categories include anecdotes and some kinds of jokes. Traditional stories, in turn, are only one category within the larger category of folklore, which also includes items such as gestures, costumes, and music. [4]

13. The main idea of this passage is

a. Myths, fables, and folktales are not the same thing, and each describes a specific type of story

b. Traditional stories can be categorized in different ways by different people

c. Cultures use myths for religious purposes, and when this is no longer true, the people forget and discard these myths

d. Myths can never become folk tales, because one is true, and the other is false

14. The terms myth and legend are

a. Categories that are synonymous with true and false

b. Categories that group traditional stories according to certain characteristics

c. Interchangeable, because both terms mean a story that is passed down from generation to generation

d. Meant to distinguish between a story that involves a hero and a cultural message and a story meant only to entertain

15. Traditional story categories not only include myths and legends, but

    a. Can also include gestures, since some cultures passed these down before the written and spoken word

    b. In addition, folklore refers to stories involving fables and fairy tales

    c. These story categories can also include folk music and traditional dress

    d. Traditional stories themselves are a part of the larger category of folklore, which may also include costumes, gestures, and music

16. This passage shows that

    a. There is a distinct difference between a myth and a legend, although both are folktales

    b. Myths are folktales, but folktales are not myths

    c. Myths, legends, and folktales play an important part in tradition and the past, and are a rich and colorful part of history

    d. Most cultures consider myths to be true

Questions 17 - 19 refer to the following passage.

How To Get A Good Nights Sleep

Sleep is just as essential for healthy living as water, air and food. Sleep allows the body to rest and replenish depleted energy levels. Sometimes we may for various reasons experience difficulty sleeping which has a serious effect on our health. Those who have prolonged sleeping problems are facing a serious medical condition and should see a qualified doctor when possible for help. Here is simple guide that can help you sleep better at night.

Try to create a natural pattern of waking up and sleeping around the same time everyday. This means avoiding going to bed too early and oversleeping past your usual wake up time. Going to bed and getting up at radically different times everyday confuses your body clock. Try to establish a natural rhythm as much as you can.

Exercises and a bit of physical activity can help you sleep better at night. If you are having problem sleeping, try to be as active as you can during the day. If you are tired from physical activity, falling asleep is a natural and easy process for your body. If you remain inactive during the day, you will find it harder to sleep properly at night. Try walking, jogging, swimming or simple stretches as you get close to your bed time.

Afternoon naps are great to refresh you during the day, but they may also keep you awake at night. If you feel sleepy during the day, get up, take a walk and get busy to keep from sleeping. Stretching is a good way to increase blood flow to the brain and keep you alert so that you don't sleep during the day. This will help you sleep better night.

A warm bath or a glass of milk in the evening can help your body relax and prepare for sleep. A cold bath will wake you up and keep you up for several hours. Also avoid eating too late before bed.

17. How would you describe this sentence?

a. A recommendation

b. An opinion

c. A fact

d. A diagnosis

18. Which of the following is an alternative title for this article?

a. Exercise and a good night's sleep

b. Benefits of a good night's sleep

c. Tips for a good night's sleep

d. Lack of sleep is a serious medical condition

19. Which of the following cannot be inferred from this article?

  a. Biking is helpful for getting a good night's sleep

  b. Mental activity is helpful for getting a good night's sleep

  c. Eating bedtime snacks is not recommended

  d. Getting up at the same time is helpful for a good night's sleep

Directions: For questions 20 to 30 you are given 2 sentences. Select the best answer that describes the relationship between the 2 sentences.

20. Plants need water to survive; however, some plants can live with very little water.

Cactuses, found in deserts where they don't get a lot of water, can survive with very little water.

  a. The second sentence gives an example.

  b. The second sentence restates an idea in the first sentence.

  c. The second sentence states an effect.

  d. The second sentence contrasts the first.

21. The Great Pyramids at Giza are the most famous ancient sites in Egypt.

The Great Pyramids at Giza are most often associated with Egypt and have been a main tourist attraction for hundreds of years.

  a. The second sentence reinforces the first.

  b. The second sentence analyzes a statement made in the first.

c. The second sentence draws a conclusion.

d. The second sentence proposes a solution.

22. Healthy people can get very sick from the flu virus and spread the virus to others.

Getting the flu vaccine is the best way to reduce the chances that you will get virus and spread it to others.

a. The second sentence reinforces the first.

b. The second sentence analyzes a statement made in the first.

c. The second sentence expands on the first.

d. The second sentence proposes a solution.

23. There is over 70% of water and less than 30% land on Earth.

Over 70% of water and less than 30% land makes up Earth.

a. The second sentence contrasts the first.

b. The second sentence states an effect.

c. The second sentence restates an idea in the first sentence.

d. The second sentence gives an example.

24. The Baltimore Ravens and the San Francisco 49ers played each other in Super Bowl XLVII.

The final score was Ravens-34 and 49ers-31, so the Ravens won the game.

a. The second sentence reinforces the first.

b. The second sentence analyzes a statement made in the first.

c. The second sentence proposes a solution.

d. The second sentence draws a conclusion.

25. The woman took her three children on an outing.

The woman took her three children on an outing to the zoo and the aquarium to see Going Bananas and Dolphin Tales, two animal shows.

    a. The second sentence reinforces the first.

    b. The second sentence analyzes a statement made in the first.

    c. The second sentence expands on the first.

    d. The second sentence proposes a solution.

26. The United States of America is the world's third largest country in terms of population.

The United States of America is one of the largest countries in terms of population.

    a. They contradict each other.

    b. They express roughly the same idea.

    c. They present problems and solutions.

    d. They establish a contrast.

27. Sophia said she is afraid of small dogs.

Sophia said she owns two teacup Yorkshire terriers.

    a. They present problems and solutions.

    b. They express roughly the same idea.

    c. They contradict each other.

    d. They establish a contrast.

28. Peggy's baby sister's, Sue, two front teeth came out.

Sue can't bite into a plum, her favorite fruit, so she cut it into bite size pieces.

    a. They express roughly the same idea.

    b. They contradict each other.

    c. They establish a contrast.

    d. They present problems and solutions.

29. An estimated 7 billion people live in the world.

There are about 7 billion people living in the world.

    a. They present problems and solutions.

    b. They contradict each other.

    c. They reinforce each other.

    d. They express roughly the same idea.

30. The cold and flu virus are both respiratory illnesses.

The common cold causes a runny nose, congestion and sore throat, but the flu virus infects the lungs, joints and intestinal tract.

    a. They repeat the same idea.

    b. They contrast each other.

    c. They reinforce each other.

    d. They provide a problem and solution.

Arithmetic

1. A map uses a scale of 1:100,000. How much distance on the ground is 3 inches on the map if the scale is in inches?

    a. 13 inches

    b. 300,000 inches

    c. 30,000 inches

    d. 333.999 inches

2. Divide 9.60 by 3.2.

    a. 2.50

    b. 3

    c. 2.3

    d. 6.4

3. Subtract 456,890 from 465,890.

    a. 9,000

    b. 7,000

    c. 8,970

    d. 8,500

4. Estimate 46,227 + 101,032.

    a. 14,700

    b. 147,000

    c. 14,700,000

    d. 104,700

5. Find the square of 25/9

    a. 5/3

    b. 3/5

    c. 7 58/81

    d. 15/2

6. Which one of the following is less than a third?

    a. 84/231

    b. 6/35

    c. 3/22

    d. b and c

7. Which of the following numbers is the largest?

    a. 1

    b. $\sqrt{2}$

    c. 3/2

    d. 4/3

8. 15/16 x 8/9 =

    a. 5/6

    b. 16/37

    c. 2/11

    d. 5/7

9. Driver B drove his car 20 km/h faster than the driver A, and driver B travelled 480 km 2 hours before driver A. What was the speed of driver A?

    a. 70

    b. 80

    c. 60

    d. 90

10. If a train travels at 72 kilometers per hour, how far will it travel in 12 seconds?

   a. 200 meters

   b. 220 meters

   c. 240 meters

   d. 260 meters

11. Tony bought 15 dozen eggs for $80. 16 eggs were broken during loading and unloading. He sold the remaining eggs for $0.54 each. What is his percent profit?

   a. 11%

   b. 11.2%

   c. 11.5%

   d. 12%

12. In a class of 83 students, 72 are present. What percent of students are absent?

   a. 12%

   b. 13%

   c. 14%

   d. 15%

13. In a local election at polling station A, 945 voters cast their vote out of 1270 registered voters. At polling station B, 860 cast their vote out of 1050 registered voters and at station C, 1210 cast their vote out of 1440 registered voters. What was the total turnout including all three polling stations?

   a. 70%

   b. 74%

   c. 76%

   d. 80%

14. Estimate 5205 ÷ 25

    a. 108

    b. 308

    c. 208

    d. 408

15. 7/15 – 3/10 =

    a. 1/6

    b. 4/5

    c. 1/7

    d. 1 1/3

16. Susan wants to buy a leather jacket that costs $545.00 and is on sale for 10% off. What is the approximate cost?

    a. $525

    b. $450

    c. $475

    d. $500

17. 11/20 ÷ 9/20 =

    a. 99/20

    b. 4 19/20

    c. 1 2/9

    d. 1 1/9

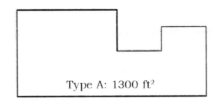

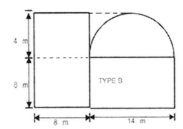

18. The price of houses in a certain subdivision is based on the total area. Susan is watching her budget and wants to choose the house with the lowest area. Which house type, A (1300 ft²) or B, should she choose if she would like the house with the lowest price?
(1cm² = 4.0ft² & π = 22/7)

    a. Type B is smaller 140 ft²

    b. Type A is smaller

    c. Type B is smaller at 855 ft²

    d. Type B is larger

19. Estimate 2009 x 108.

    a. 110,000

    b. 2,0000

    c. 21,000

    d. 210,000

20. Simplify 0.12 + 1 2/5 − 1 3/5

    a. 1 1/25

    b. 1 3/25

    c. 1 2/5

    d. 2 3/5

Algebra

21. Using the quadratic formula, solve the quadratic equation: $0.9x^2 + 1.8x - 2.7 = 0$

    a. 1 and 3

    b. -3 and 1

    c. -3 and -1

    d. -1 and 3

22. Subtract polynomial $5x^3 + x^2 + x + 5$ from $4x^3 - 2x^2 - 10$.

    a. $-x^3 - 3x^2 - x - 15$

    b. $9x^3 - 3x^2 - x - 15$

    c. $-x^3 - x^2 + x - 5$

    d. $9x^3 - x^2 + x + 5$

23. Find x and y from the following system of equations:

(4x + 5y)/3 = ((x − 3y)/2) + 4
(3x + y)/2 = ((2x + 7y)/3) −1

    a. (1, 3)

    b. (2, 1)

    c. (1, 1)

    d. (0, 1)

24. Using the factoring method, solve the quadratic equation: $x^2 + 12x - 13 = 0$

    a. -13 and 1

    b. -13 and -1

    c. 1 and 13

    d. -1 and 13

25. Using the quadratic formula, solve the quadratic equation: $((x^2 + 4x + 4) + (x^2 - 4x + 4)) / (x^2 - 4) = 0$.

    a. It has infinite numbers of solutions

    b. 0 and 1

    c. It has no solutions

    d. 0

26. Turn the following expression into a simple polynomial:

$5(3x^2 - 2) - x^2(2 - 3x)$

    a. $3x^3 + 17x^2 - 10$

    b. $3x^3 + 13x^2 + 10$

    c. $-3x^3 - 13x^2 - 10$

    d. $3x^3 + 13x^2 - 10$

27. Solve $(x^3 + 2)(x^2 - x) - x^5$.

    a. $2x^5 - x^4 + 2x^2 - 2x$

    b. $-x^4 + 2x^2 - 2x$

    c. $-x^4 - 2x^2 - 2x$

    d. $-x^4 + 2x^2 + 2x$

28. 9ab² + 8ab² =

    a. ab²

    b. 17ab²

    c. 17

    d. 17a²b²

29. Factor the polynomial x² - 7x - 30.

    a. (x + 15)(x - 2)

    b. (x + 10)(x - 3)

    c. (x - 10)(x + 3)

    d. (x - 15)(x + 2)

30. If a and b are real numbers, solve the following equation: (a + 2)x - b = -2 + (a + b)x

    a. -1

    b. 0

    c. 1

    d. 2

31. If A = -2x⁴ + x² - 3x , B = x⁴ - x³ + 5 and C = x⁴ + 2x³ + 4x + 5, find A + B - C.

    a. $x^3 + x^2 + x + 10$

    b. $-3x^3 + x^2 - 7x + 10$

    c. $-2x^4 - 3x^3 + x^2 - 7x$

    d. $-3x^4 + x^3 + x^2 - 7x$

32. (4Y³ – 2Y²) + (7Y² + 3y - y) =

    a. $4y^3 + 9y^2 + 4y$

    b. $5y^3 + 5y^2 + 3y$

    c. $4y^3 + 7y^2 + 2y$

    d. $4y^3 + 5y^2 + 2y$

33. Turn the following expression into a simple polynomial: $1 - x(1 - x(1 - x))$

    a. $x^3 + x^2 - x + 1$

    b. $-x^3 - x^2 + x + 1$

    c. $-x^3 + x^2 - x + 1$

    d. $x^3 + x^2 - x - 1$

34. $7(2y + 8) + 1 - 4(y + 5) =$

    a. $10y + 36$

    b. $10y + 77$

    c. $18y + 37$

    d. $10y + 37$

35. Richard gives 's' amount of salary to each of his 'n' employees weekly. If he has 'x' amount of money then how many days he can employ these 'n' employees.

    a. sx/7n

    b. 7x/nx

    c. nx/7s

    d. 7x/ns

36. Factor the polynomial $x^2 - 3x - 4$.

    a. $(x + 1)(x - 4)$

    b. $(x - 1)(x + 4)$

    c. $(x - 1)(x - 4)$

    d. $(x + 1)(x + 4)$

37. Solve the inequality: $(2x + 1)/(2x - 1) < 1$.

    a. $(-2, + \infty)$

    b. $(1, + \infty)$

    c. $(-\infty, -2)$

    d. $(-\infty, 1/2)$

38. Using the quadratic formula, solve the quadratic equation:

$(a^2 - b^2)x^2 + 2ax + 1 = 0$

    a. $a/(a + b)$ and $b/(a + b)$

    b. $1/(a + b)$ and $a/(a + b)$

    c. $a/(a + b)$ and $a/(a - b)$

    d. $-1/(a + b)$ and $-1/(a - b)$

39. Turn the following expression into a simple polynomial: $(a + b)(x + y) + (a - b)(x - y) - (ax + by)$

    a. $ax + by$

    b. $ax - by$

    c. $ax^2 + by^2$

    d. $ax^2 - by^2$

40. Given polynomials $A = 4x^5 - 2x^2 + 3x - 2$ and $B = -3x^4 - 5x^2 - 4x + 5$, find $A + B$.

    a. $x^5 - 3x^2 - x - 3$

    b. $4x^5 - 3x^4 + 7x^2 + x + 3$

    c. $4x^5 - 3x^4 - 7x^2 - x + 3$

    d. $4x^5 - 3x^4 - 7x^2 - x - 7$

College Level

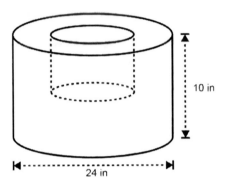

24 in

Note: Figure not drawn to scale

41. What is the volume of the above solid made by a hollow cylinder that is half the size (in all dimensions) of the larger cylinder?

    a. 1440 π in³

    b. 1260 π in³

    c. 1040 π in³

    d. 960 π in³

42. Find x if log$_{1/2}$x = 4.

    a. 16

    b. 8

    c. 1/8

    d. 1/16

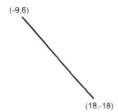

(-9,6)

(18,-18)

43. What is the slope of the line above?

    a. -8/9
    b. 9/8
    c. -9/8
    d. 8/9

44. If the sequence $\{a_n\}$ is defined by $a_{n+1} = 1 - a_n$ and $a_2 = 6$, find a_4.

    a. 2
    b. 1
    c. 6
    d. -1

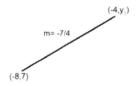

(-4,y₁)

m= -7/4

(-8,7)

45. With the data given above, what is the value of y_1?

    a. 0
    b. -7
    c. 7
    d. 8

46. The area of a rectangle is 20 cm². If one side increases by 1 cm and other by 2 cm, the area of the new rectangle is 35 cm². Find the sides of the original rectangle.

> a. (4,8)
>
> b. (4,5)
>
> c. (2.5,8)
>
> d. b and c

47. Solve $\log_{10} 10{,}000 = x$.

> a. 2
>
> b. 4
>
> c. 3
>
> d. 6

(18,12)

(9,-6)

48. What is the distance between the two points?

> a. ≈19
>
> b. 20
>
> c. ≈21
>
> d. ≈22

49. If in the right triangle, a is 12 and sinα=12/13, find cosα.

    a. -5/13

    b. -1/13

    c. 1/13

    d. 5/13

50. Find the solution for the following linear equation:
1/(4x - 2) = 5/6

    a. 0.2

    b. 0.4

    c. 0.6

    d. 0.8

(-1,2)

(-4,-4)

51. What is the slope of the line above?

    a. 1

    b. 2

    c. 3

    d. -2

52. How much water can be stored in a cylindrical container 5 meters in diameter and 12 meters high?

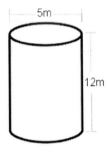

5m

12m

    a. 235.65 m³

    b. 223.65 m³

    c. 240.65 m³

    d. 252.65 m³

53. If members of the sequence {an} are represented by $a_{n+1} = - a_{n-1}$ and $a_2 = 3$ and, find $a_3 + a_4$.

    a. 2

    b. 3

    c. 0

    d. -2

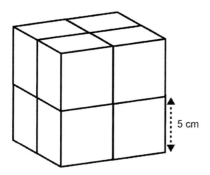

Note: Figure not drawn to scale

54. Assuming the figure above is composed of cubes, what is the volume?

     a. 125 cm^3

     b. 875 cm^3

     c. 1000 cm^3

     d. 500 cm^3

55. Solve

$x \sqrt{5} - y = \sqrt{5}$
$x - y \sqrt{5} = 5$

     a. $(0, -\sqrt{5})$

     b. $(0, \sqrt{5})$

     c. $(-\sqrt{5}, 0)$

     d. $(\sqrt{5}, 0)$

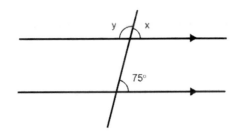

56. What is the value of the angle y?

    a. 25°

    b. 15°

    c. 30°

    d. 105°

57. Using the right triangle's legs, calculate (sinα + cosβ)/(tgα + ctgβ).

    a. a/b

    b. b/c

    c. b/a

    d. a/c

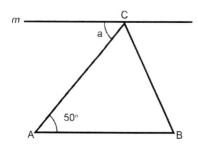

58. If the line *m* is parallel to the side AB of △ABC, what is angle *a*?

    a. 130°

    b. 25°

    c. 65°

    d. 50°

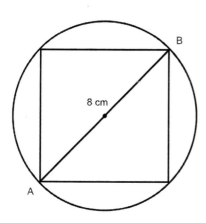

Note: figure not drawn to scale

59. What is area of the circle above?

    a. 4π cm^2

    b. 12π cm^2

    c. 10π cm^2

    d. 16π cm^2

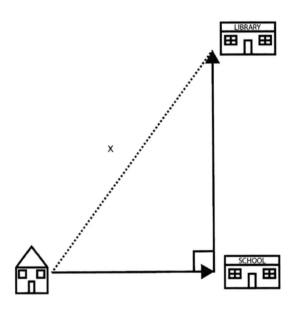

60. Every day starting from his home Peter travels due east 3 kilometers to the school. After school he travels due north 4 kilometers to the library. What is the distance between Peter's home and the library?

    a. 15 km

    b. 10 km

    c. 5 km

    d. 12 ½ km

Sentence Skills

Directions: Select the best version of the underlined portion of the sentence

1. <u>Who</u> won first place in the Western Division?

    a. Whom won first place in the Western Division?

    b. Which won first place in the Western Division?

    c. What won first place in the Western Division?

    d. No change is necessary?

2. There are now several ways to listen to music, including radio, CDs, and Mp3 files <u>which</u> you can download onto an MP3 player.

    a. There are now several ways to listen to music, including radio, CDs, and Mp3 files on which you can download onto an MP3 player.

    b. There are now several ways to listen to music, including radio, CDs, and Mp3 files who you can download onto an MP3 player.

    c. There are now several ways to listen to music, including radio, CDs, and Mp3 files whom you can download onto an MP3 player.

    d. No change is necessary.

3. As the tallest monument in the United States, the St. Louis Arch <u>was rose to an impressive 630 feet</u>.

    a. As the tallest monument in the United States, the St. Louis Arch has rose to an impressive 630 feet.

    b. As the tallest monument in the United States, the St. Louis Arch is risen to an impressive 630 feet.

    c. As the tallest monument in the United States, the St. Louis Arch rises to an impressive 630 feet.

    d. No change is necessary.

4. The tired, old woman should <u>lain</u> on the sofa.

    a. The tired, old woman should lie on the sofa.

    b. The tired, old woman should lays on the sofa.

    c. The tired, old woman should laid on the sofa.

    d. No changes are necessary.

5. Did the students understand that Thanksgiving always <u>fallen</u> on the fourth Thursday in November?

    a No change is necessary.

    b. Did the students understand that Thanksgiving always falling on the fourth Thursday in November.

    c. Did the students understand that Thanksgiving always has fell on the fourth Thursday in November.

    d. Did the students understand that Thanksgiving always falls on the fourth Thursday in November.

6. Collecting stamps, <u>build models</u>, and listening to shortwave radio were Rick's main hobbies.

    a. Collecting stamps, building models, and listening to shortwave radio were Rick's main hobbies.

    b. Collecting stamps, to build models, and listening to shortwave radio were Rick's main hobbies.

    c. Collecting stamps, having built models, and listening to shortwave radio were Rick's main hobbies.

    d. No change is necessary.

7. This morning, <u>after the kids will leave for school</u> and before the sun came up, my mother makes herself a cup of cocoa.

a. This morning, after the kids had left for school and before the sun came up, my mother makes herself a cup of cocoa.

b. This morning, after the kids leave for school and before the sun came up, my mother makes herself a cup of cocoa.

c. This morning, after the kids have left for school and before the sun came up, my mother makes herself a cup of cocoa.

d. No change is necessary.

8. Elaine promised to bring the camera <u>to me</u> at the mall yesterday.

a. Elaine promised to bring the camera by me at the mall yesterday.

b. Elaine promised to bring the camera with me at the mall yesterday.

c. Elaine promised to bring the camera at me at the mall yesterday.

d. No changes are necessary.

9. Last night, he <u>laid</u> the sleeping bag down beside my mattress.

a. Last night, he lay the sleeping bag down beside my mattress.

b. Last night, he lain

c. Last night, he has laid

d. No change is necessary.

10. I would have bought the shirt for you <u>if I know</u> you liked it.

> a. I would have bought the shirt for you if I had known you liked it.
>
> b. I would have bought the shirt for you if I have known you liked it.
>
> c. I would have bought the shirt for you if I would know you liked it.
>
> d. No change is necessary.

For questions 11 - 20, rewrite the sentence given keeping the same meaning.

11. Though less spectacular, lunar eclipses occur more frequently than the solar ones.

Rewrite, beginning with

Lunar eclipses occur more frequently than the solar ones,

The next words will be

> a. and they are less spectacular
>
> b. though less spectacular
>
> c. but they are less spectacular
>
> d. but it is less spectacular

12. It is unwise to drink too many cups of coffee, but green tea is always a healthy option.

Rewrite, beginning with

Unlike coffee,

The next words will be

  a. it is always healthy to

  b. you can always drink

  c. green tea is always

  d. it is unwise to

13. Shark teeth are very sharp, but they fall out easily.

Rewrite, beginning with

Even though they are very sharp,

The next words will be

  a. shark teeth fall out

  b. falling out easily

  c. but shark teeth fall out

  d. it is easy that

14. Missing their two best players, the team will not be able to score as easily.

Rewrite, beginning with

It is not as easy for the team to score

The next words will be

  a. without their two best

  b. and their two best

  c. being absent their two best

  d. but since their two best

15. Antoine ate the appetizer and then went on to the main course.

Rewrite, beginning with

Before going on to the main course,

The next words will be

    a. Antoine ate

    b. eating first the main

    c. and then Antoine

    d. it was the main course

16. Skating along the boardwalk, Kathy spotted her friend in the surf.

Rewrite, beginning with

Kathy spotted her friend in the surf

The next words will be

    a. after skating along the

    b. and then skated along the

    c. along the boardwalk

    d. as she was skating along the

17. As omnivores, bears eat berries and other animals.

Rewrite, beginning with

Eating berries and other animals,

The next words will be

    a. because omnivores

    b. bears are omnivores

    c. although omnivores

    d. bears are omnivores

18. Volcanoes hardly ever erupt, and even more rarely do they endanger human life.

Rewrite, beginning with

Volcanoes endanger human life even more rarely

The next words will be

    a. and erupt

    b. than they erupt

    c. although erupting

    d. but then they erupt

19. Not having studied until the morning of the test, Jeremy was tired and anxious as he wrote down his answers.

Rewrite, beginning with

Jeremy was tired and anxious as he wrote down his answers

The next words will be

    a. although he had not studied

    b. not having studied

    c. because he had not studied

    d. until the morning of the test

20. Claire enjoyed the film, but she wished it had ended more happily.

Rewrite, beginning with

Wishing it had ended more happily,

The next words will be

     a. Claire nonetheless enjoyed

     b. Claire enjoyed

     c. the film was nonetheless enjoyed

     d. although enjoying the film

Answer Key

Reading Comprehension

1. A
Secede most nearly means to break away from because the 11 states wanted to leave the United States and form their own country.

Option B is incorrect because the states were not accomplishing anything. Option C is incorrect because the states were trying to leave the USA not join it. Option D is incorrect because the states seceded before they lost the war.

2. B
Look at the dates in the passage. The shots were fired on April 12 and Congress declared war on April 14.

Option C is incorrect because the passage states that Lincoln was against slavery. Option D is incorrect because it never mentions who was or was not at Fort Sumter.

3. C
The passage states that Lee surrendered to Grant after the capture of the capital of the Confederacy, which is Richmond.

Option A is incorrect because the war continued for 2 years after Gettysburg. Option B is incorrect because that battle is not mentioned in the passage. Option D is incorrect because the capture of the capital occurred after the march to the sea.

4. A
When the passage said that the North had *abolished* slavery, it implies that slaves were no longer allowed in the North. In essence slavery was banned.

Option B makes no sense relative to the context of the passage. Option C is incorrect because we know the North was fighting against slavery, not for it. Option D is incorrect because slavery is not a tangible thing that can be destroyed. It is a practice that had to be outlawed or banned.

5. A
We can infer that, an electrical discharge in the clouds causes lightning.

The passage tells us that, "Lightning occurs when static electricity inside clouds builds up and causes an electrical charge,"

6. C
Being struck by lightning means, a ninety percent chance of surviving the strike.

From the passage, "statistics show that 90% of victims survive a lightning blast."

7. A
We know that lightning is static electricity from the third sentence in the passage. We also know that water droplets colliding with ice crystals cause static electricity. Therefore, Lightning is caused by water droplets colliding with ice crystals.

8. A
Low blood sugar occurs both in diabetics and healthy adults.

9. B
None of the statements are the author's opinion.

10. A
The author's purpose is the inform.

11. A
The only statement that is not a detail is, "A doctor can diagnosis this medical condition by asking the patient questions and testing."

12. B
This passage describes the different categories for traditional stories. The other choices are facts from the passage, not the main idea of the passage. The main idea of a passage will

always be the most general statement. For example, Choice A, Myths, fables, and folktales are not the same thing, and each describes a specific type of story. This is a true statement from the passage, but not the main idea of the passage, since the passage also talks about how some cultures may classify a story as a myth and others as a folktale. The statement, from choice B, Traditional stories can be categorized in different ways by different people, is a more general statement that describes the passage.

13. B
Choice B is the best choice, categories that group traditional stories according to certain characteristics.

Choices A and C are false and can be eliminated right away. Choice D is designed to confuse. Choice D may be true, but it is not mentioned in the passage.

14. D
The best answer is D, traditional stories themselves are a part of the larger category of folklore, which may also include costumes, gestures, and music.

All the other choices are false. Traditional stories are part of the larger category of Folklore, which includes other things, not the other way around.

15. A
The sentence is a recommendation.

16. C
Tips for a good night's sleep is the best alternative title for this article.

17. B
Mental activity is helpful for a good night's sleep is can not be inferred from this article.

18. C
This question tests the reader's vocabulary and contextualization skills. A may or may not be true, but focuses on the wrong function of the word "give" and ignores the rest of the sentence, which is more relevant to what the passage is discussing. B and D may also be selected if the reader depends

too literally on the word "give," failing to grasp the more abstract function of the word that is the focus of answer C, which also properly acknowledges the entirety of the passage and its meaning.

19. A
Navy Seals are the maritime component of the United States Special Operations Command (USSOCOM).

20. A
Plants need water to survive; however, some plants can live with very little water.

Cactuses, found in deserts where they don't get a lot of water, can survive with very little water.

The second sentence gives an example of a plant that can live with very little water.

21. A
The Great Pyramids at Giza are the most famous ancient sites in Egypt.

The Great Pyramids at Giza are most often associated with Egypt and have been a main tourist attraction for hundreds of years.

The second sentence reinforces the first with supporting details.

22. D
Healthy people can get very sick from the flu virus and spread the virus to others.

Getting the flu vaccine is the best way to reduce the chances that you will get virus and spread it to others.

The second sentence proposes a solution for the problem mentioned in the first sentence.

23. C
There is over 70% of water and less than 30% land on Earth.

Over 70% of water and less than 30% land makes up Earth.

The second sentence restates an idea in the first sentence.

24. D
The Baltimore Ravens and the San Francisco 49ers played each other in Super Bowl XLVII.

The score was Ravens-34 and 49ers-31.

The second sentence reveals the outcome (results) of the game.

25. C
The woman took her three children on an outing.

The woman took her three children on an outing to the zoo and the aquarium to see Going Bananas and Dolphin Tales, two animal shows.

The second sentence expands on the first sentence because it expresses in greater detail where the mother took her children.

26. B
The United States of America is the world's third largest country in terms of population.

The United States of America is one of the largest countries in terms of population.

The second sentence expresses roughly the same idea.

27. C
Sophia said she is afraid of small dogs.

Sophia said she owns two teacup Yorkshire terriers.

The two sentences contradict each other.

28. D
Peggy's baby sister's, Sue, two front teeth came out.

Sue can't bite into a plum, her favorite fruit, so she cut it into bite size pieces.

The second sentence provides a problem and solution.

29. D
An estimated 7 billion people live in the world.

There are about 7 billion people living in the world.

The second sentence expresses roughly the same idea.

30. B
The cold and flu virus are both respiratory illnesses.

The common cold causes a runny nose, congestion and sore throat, but the flu virus infects the lungs, joints and intestinal tract.

They contrast each other.

The second sentence describes the differences between the cold and flu virus whereas the first compares their similarities.

Arithmetic

1. B
1 inch on map = 100,000 inches on ground. So 3 inches on map = 3 x 100,000 = 300,000 inches on ground.

2. B
9.60/3.2 = 3

3. A
465,890 - 456,890 = 9,000.

4. B
46,227 + 101,032 is about 147,000. The exact answer is 147,259.

5. C
$(25/9)^2 = 625/81$

6. D
$84/231 = 12/33 > 1/3$
$6/35 = 1/5 < 1/3$
$3/22 = 1/7 < 1/3$

7. B
$\sqrt{2}$ is the largest number.
Here are the choices:

    a. 1

    b. $\sqrt{2} = 1.414$

    c. $3/22 = .1563$

    d. $4/3 = 1.33$

8. A
First cancel out $15/16 \times 8/9$ to get $5/2 \times 1/3$, then multiply numerators and denominators to get $5/6$.

9. B
We are told that driver B is 20 km/h faster than driver A. So:
$V_B = V_A + 20$ where V is the velocity. Also, driver B travelled 480 km 2 hours before driver A. So:

$x = 480$ km

$t_A - 2 = t_B$ where t is the time. Now we know the relationship between A and B drivers in terms of time and velocity. We need to write an equation only depending on V_A (the speed of driver A) which we are asked to find.

Since distance = velocity•time: $480 = V_A•t_A = V_B•t_B$

$480 = (V_A + 20)(t_A - 2)$

$480 = (V_A + 20)(480/V_A - 2)$

$480 = 480 - 2V_A + 20•480/V_A - 40$

$0 = -2V_A + 9600/V_A - 40$ ... Multiplying the equation by V_A eliminates the denominator:

$2V_A^2 + 40V_A - 9600 = 0$ ... Simplifying the equation by 2:

$V_A^2 + 20V_A - 4800 = 0$

$V_{A1,2} = [- 20 \pm \sqrt{(400 + 4 \cdot 4800)}] / 2$

$V_{A1,2} = [- 20 \pm 140] / 2$

$V_A = [-20 - 140]/2 = -80$ km/h and $V_A = [-20 + 140]/2 = 60$ km/h

We need to check our answers. It is easy to make a table:

t_A	V_A	V_B	t_B	$t_A - t_B$
480/80 = 6	-80	-80 - 20 = -100 B is 20 km/h faster than A. - sign only mentions the direction of the velocity. For magnitude, we need to add -20.	480/100 = 4.8	6 - 4.8 = 1.2 This should be 2!
480/60 = 8	60	60 + 20 = 80	480/80 = 6	8 - 6 = 2 This is correct !

So, $V_A = 60$ km/h is the only answer satisfying the question.

10. C

1 hour is equal to 3,600 seconds and 1 kilometer is equal to 1000 meters.

Since this train travels 72 kilometers per hour, this means that it covers 72,000 meters in 3,600 seconds.

If it travels 72,000 meters in 3,600 seconds

It travels x meters in 12 seconds

By cross multiplication: x = 72,000 • 12 / 3,600

x = 240 meters

11. A

Let us first mention the money Tony spent: $80

Now we need to find the money Tony earned:

He had 15 dozen eggs = 15•12 = 180 eggs. 16 eggs were broken. So,

Remaining number of eggs that Tony sold = 180 – 16 = 164.

Total amount he earned for selling 164 eggs = 164•0.54 = $88.56.

As a summary, he spent $80 and earned $88.56.

The profit is the difference: 88.56 - 80 = $8.56

Percentage profit is found by proportioning the profit to the money he spent:

8.56•100/80 = 10.7%

Checking the answers, we round 10.7 to the nearest whole number: 11%

12. B
Number of absent students = 83 – 72 = 11

Percentage of absent students is found by proportioning the number of absent students to total number of students in the class = 11•100/83 = 13.25

Checking the answers, we round 13.25 to the nearest whole number: 13%

13. D
To find the total turnout in all three polling stations, we need to proportion the number of voters to the number of all registered voters.

Number of total voters = 945 + 860 + 1210 = 3015

Number of total registered voters = 1270 + 1050 + 1440 = 3760

Percentage turnout over all three polling stations =
3015•100/3760 = 80.19%

Checking the answers, we round 80.19 to the nearest whole number: 80%

14. C
The approximate answer to 5205 ÷ 25 is 208. The exact answer is 208.2.

15. A
A common denominator is needed, a number which both 15 and 10 will divide into. So 14-9/30 = 5/30 = 1/6

16. D
The jacket costs $545.00 so we can round up to $550. 10% of $550 is 55. We can round down to $50, which is easier to work with. $550 - $50 is $500. The jacket will cost about $500.

The actual cost is 545 - 54.50 = 490.50.

17. C
11/20 x 20/9 = 11/1 x 1/9 = 11/9 = 1 2/9

18. C
Area of Type B consists of two rectangles and a half circle. We can find these three areas and sum them up in order to find the total area:

Area of the left rectangle: $(4 + 8) \cdot 8 = 96$ m^2

Area of the right rectangle: $14 \cdot 8 = 112$ m^2

The diameter of the circle is equal to 14 m. So, the radius is 14/2 = 7:

Area of the half circle = $(1/2) \cdot \pi r^2 = (1/2) \cdot (22/7) \cdot (7)^2 = (1 \cdot 22 \cdot 49)/(2 \cdot 7) = 77$ m^2

Area of Type B = 96 + 112 + 77 = 285 m^2

Converting this area to ft^2: 285 m^2 = $285 \cdot 10.76$ ft^2 = 3066.6 ft^2

Type B is (3066.6 - 1300 = 1766.6 ft^2) 1766.6 ft^2 larger than type A.

19. D
2009 x 108 is about 210,000. The exact answer is 216,972.

20. B
0.12 + 2/5 + 3/5, Convert decimal to fraction to get 3/25 + 2/5 + 3/5, = (3 + 10 + 15)/25, = 28/25 = 1 3/25

Algebra

21. B
To solve the equation, we need the equation in the form $ax^2 + bx + c = 0$.
$0.9x^2 + 1.8x - 2.7 = 0$ is already in this form.

The quadratic formula to find the roots of a quadratic equation is:

$x_{1,2} = (-b \pm \sqrt{\Delta}) / 2a$ where $\Delta = b^2 - 4ac$ and is called the discriminant of the quadratic equation.

In our question, the equation is $0.9x^2 + 1.8x - 2.7 = 0$. To eliminate the decimals, let us multiply the equation by 10:

$9x^2 + 18x - 27 = 0$ ... This equation can be simplified by 9 since each term contains 9:

$x^2 + 2x - 3 = 0$

By remembering the form $ax^2 + bx + c = 0$:

$a = 1, b = 2, c = -3$

So, we can find the discriminant first, and then the roots of the equation:

$\Delta = b^2 - 4ac = (2)^2 - 4 \bullet 1 \bullet (-3) = 4 + 12 = 16$

$x_{1,2} = (-b \pm \sqrt{\Delta}) / 2a = (-2 \pm \sqrt{16}) / 2 = (-2 \pm 4) / 2$

This means that the roots are,

$x_1 = (-2 - 4)/2 = -3$ and $x_2 = (-2 + 4)/2 = 1$

22. A
We are asked to subtract polynomials. By paying attention to the sign distribution; we write the polynomials and operate:

$4x^3 - 2x^2 - 10 - (5x^3 + x^2 + x + 5) = 4x^3 - 2x^2 - 10 - 5x^3 - x^2 - x - 5$

$= 4x^3 - 5x^3 - 2x^2 - x^2 - x - 10 - 5$ ... similar terms written together to ease summing/substituting.

$= -x^3 - 3x^2 - x - 15$

23. C

First, we need to arrange the two equations to obtain the form ax + by = c. We see that there are 3 and 2 in the denominators of both equations. If we equate all at 6, then we can cancel all 6 in the denominators and have straight equations:

Equate all denominators at 6:

2(4x + 5y)/6 = 3(x - 3y)/6 + 4•6/6 ... Now we can cancel 6 in the denominators:

8x + 10y = 3x - 9y + 24 ... We can collect x and y terms on left side of the equation:

8x + 10y - 3x + 9y = 24

5x + 19y = 24 ... Equation (I)

Let us arrange the second equation:

3(3x + y)/6 = 2(2x + 7y)/6 - 1•6/6 ... Now we can cancel 6 in the denominators:

9x + 3y = 4x + 14y - 6 ... We can collect x and y terms on left side of the equation:

9x + 3y - 4x - 14y = -6

5x - 11y = -6 ... Equation (II)

Now, we have two equations and two unknowns x and y. By writing the two equations one under the other and operating, we can find one unknowns first, and find the other next:

5x + 19y = 24

-1/ 5x - 11y = -6 ... If we substitute this equation from the upper one, 5x cancels -5x:

5x + 19y = 24

-5x + 11y = 6 ... Summing side-by-side:

5x - 5x + 19y + 11y = 24 + 6

30y = 30 ... Dividing both sides by 30:

y = 1

Inserting y = 1 into either of the equations, we can find the value of x. Choosing equation I:

5x + 19•1 = 24

5x = 24 - 19

5x = 5 ... Dividing both sides by 5:

x = 1

So, x = 1 and y = 1 is the solution; it is shown as (1, 1).

24. A

x^2 + 12x - 13 = 0 ... We try to separate the middle term 12x to find common factors with x^2 and -13 separately:

x^2 + 13x - x - 13 = 0 ... Here, we see that x is a common factor for x^2 and 13x, and -1 is a common factor for -x and -13:

x(x + 13) - 1(x + 13) = 0 ... Here, we have x times x + 13 and -1 times x + 13 summed up. This means that we have x - 1 times x + 13:

(x - 1)(x + 13) = 0

This is true when either or, both of the expressions in the parenthesis are equal to zero:

x - 1 = 0 ... x = 1

x + 13 = 0 ... x = -13

1 and -13 are the solutions for this quadratic equation.

25. C

First, we need to simplify the equation:
$((x^2 + 4x + 4) + (x^2 - 4x + 4)) / (x^2 - 4) = 0$

$(x^2 + 4x + 4 + x^2 - 4x + 4) / (x^2 - 4) = 0$ ... 4x and -4x in the numerator cancel each other.

Note that x^2 - 4 is two square difference and is equal to $x^2 - 2^2 = (x - 2)(x + 2)$:

$(2x^2 + 8)/((x - 2)(x + 2)) = 0$

The denominator tells us that if x - 2 or x + 2 equals to zero, there will be no solution. So, we will need to eliminate x = 2 and x = -2 from our solution which will be found considering the numerator:

$2x^2 + 8 = 0$

$2(x^2 + 4) = 0$

$x^2 + 4 = 0$

$x^2 = -4$ ... We know that, a square cannot be equal to a negative number. Solution for the square root of -4 is not a real number, so this equation has no solution.

26. D
We need to distribute the factors to the terms inside the related parenthesis:

$5(3x^2 - 2) - x^2(2 - 3x) = 15x^2 - 10 - (2x^2 - 3x^3)$

$= 15x^2 - 10 - 2x^2 + 3x^3$

$= 3x^3 + 15x^2 - 2x^2 - 10$ ... similar terms written together to ease summing/substituting.

$= 3x^3 + 13x^2 - 10$

27. B
We need to distribute the factors to the terms inside the related parenthesis:

$(x^3 + 2)(x^2 - x) - x^5 = x^5 - x^4 + (2x^2 - 2x) - x^5$

$= x^5 - x^4 + 2x^2 - 2x - x^5$

$= x^5 - x^5 - x^4 + 2x^2 - 2x$ ... similar terms written together to ease summing/substituting.

$= -x^4 + 2x^2 - 2x$

28. B
To simplify the expression, we need to find common factors. We see that both terms contain the term ab^2. So, we can take this term out of each term as a factor:

$9ab^2 + 8ab^2 = (9 + 8)\ ab^2 = 17ab^2$

29. C

$x^2 - 7x - 30 = 0$ ... We try to separate the middle term $-7x$ to find common factors with x^2 and -30 separately:

$x^2 - 10x + 3x - 30 = 0$ ... Here, we see that x is a common factor for x^2 and $-10x$, and 3 is a common factor for $3x$ and -30:

$x(x - 10) + 3(x - 10) = 0$ ... Here, we have x times x - 10 and 3 times x - 10 summed up. This means that we have x + 3 times x - 10:

$(x + 3)(x - 10) = 0$ or $(x - 10)(x + 3) = 0$

30. A

We need to simplify the equation by distributing factors and then collecting x terms on one side, and the others on the other side:

$(a + 2)x - b = -2 + (a + b)x$

$ax + 2x - b = -2 + ax + bx$

$ax + 2x - ax - bx = -2 + b$ ... ax and -ax cancel each other:

$2x - bx = -2 + b$ ... we take -1 as a factor on the right side:

$(2 - b)x = -(2 - b)$

$x = -(2 - b)/(2 - b)$ ... Simplifying by 2 - b:

$x = -1$

31. C

We are asked to find A + B - C. By paying attention to the sign distribution; we write the polynomials and operate:

$A + B - C = (-2x^4 + x^2 - 3x) + (x^4 - x^3 + 5) - (x^4 + 2x^3 + 4x + 5)$

$= -2x^4 + x^2 - 3x + x^4 - x^3 + 5 - x^4 - 2x^3 - 4x - 5$

$= -2x^4 + x^4 - x^4 - x^3 - 2x^3 + x^2 - 3x - 4x + 5 - 5$ ... similar terms written together to ease summing/substituting.

$= -2x^4 - 3x^3 + x^2 - 7x$

32. D

To simplify, we remove parenthesis:

$(4y^3 - 2y^2) + (7y^2 + 3y - y) = 4y^3 - 2y^2 + 7y^2 + 3y - y$ ... Then, we operate within similar terms:

$= 4y^3 + (-2 + 7)y^2 + (3 - 1)y = 4y^3 + 5y^2 + 2y$

33. C

To obtain a polynomial, we should remove the parenthesis by distributing the related factors to the terms inside the parenthesis:
$1 - x(1 - x(1 - x)) = 1 - x(1 - (x - x•x)) = 1 - x(1 - x + x^2)$

$= 1 - (x - x•x + x•x^2) = 1 - x + x^2 - x^3$ ... Writing this result in descending order of powers:

$= -x^3 + x^2 - x + 1$

34. D

To simplify the expression, remove the parenthesis by distributing the related factors to the terms inside the parenthesis:

$7(2y + 8) + 1 - 4(y + 5) = (7•2y + 7•8) + 1 - (4•y + 4•5)$

$= 14y + 56 + 1 - 4y - 20$

$= 14y - 4y + 56 + 1 - 20$ ... similar terms written together to ease summing/substituting.

$= 10y + 37$

35. D

We understand that each of the n employees earn s amount of salary weekly. This means that one employee earns s salary weekly. So; Richard has ns amount of money to employ n employees for a week.

We are asked to find the number of days n employees can be employed with x amount of money. We can do simple direct proportion:

If Richard can employ n employees for 7 days with ns amount of money,

Richard can employ n employees for y days with x amount of money ... y is the number of days we need to find.

We can do cross multiplication:

y = (x•7)/(ns)

y = 7x/ns

36. A
x^2 - 3x - 4 ... We try to separate the middle term -3x to find common factors with x^2 and -4 separately:

x^2 + x - 4x - 4 ... Here, we see that x is a common factor for x^2 and x, and -4 is a common factor for -4x and -4:

= x(x + 1) - 4(x + 1) ... Here, we have x times x + 1 and -4 times x + 1 summed up. This means that we have x - 4 times x + 1:

= (x - 4)(x + 1) or (x + 1)(x - 4)

37. D
We need to simplify and have x alone and on one side in order to solve the inequality:

(2x + 1)/(2x - 1) < 1

(2x + 1)/(2x - 1) - 1 < 0 ... We need to write the left side at the common denominator 2x - 1:

(2x + 1)/(2x - 1) - (2x - 1)/(2x - 1) < 0

(2x + 1 - 2x + 1)/(2x - 1) < 0 ... 2x and -2x terms cancel each other in the numerator:

2/(2x - 1) < 0

2 is a positive number; so,

2x - 1 < 0

2x < 1

x < 1/2 ... This means that x should be smaller than 1/2 and not equal to 1/2. This is shown as (-∞, 1/2).

38. D
To solve the equation, we need the equation in the form $ax^2 + bx + c = 0$.
$(a^2 - b^2)x^2 + 2ax + 1 = 0$ is already in this form.

The quadratic formula to find the roots of a quadratic equation is:

$x_{1,2} = (-b \pm \sqrt{\Delta}) / 2a$ where $\Delta = b^2 - 4ac$ and is called the discriminant of the quadratic equation.

In our question, the equation is $(a^2 - b^2)x^2 + 2ax + 1 = 0$.

By remembering the form $ax^2 + bx + c = 0$: $a = a^2 - b^2$, $b = 2a$, $c = 1$

So, we can find the discriminant first, and then the roots of the equation:

$\Delta = b^2 - 4ac = (2a)^2 - 4(a^2 - b^2) \cdot 1 = 4a^2 - 4a^2 + 4b^2 = 4b^2$

$x_{1,2} = (-b \pm \sqrt{\Delta}) / 2a = (-2a \pm \sqrt{4b^2}) / (2(a^2 - b^2)) = (-2a \pm 2b) / (2(a^2 - b^2))$

$= 2(-a \pm b) / (2(a^2 - b^2))$ ... We can simplify by 2:

$= (-a \pm b) / (a^2 - b^2)$

This means that the roots are,

$x_1 = (-a - b) / (a^2 - b^2)$ ... $a^2 - b^2$ is two square differences:

$x_1 = -(a + b) / ((a - b)(a + b))$ ... $(a + b)$ terms cancel each other:

$x_1 = -1/(a - b)$

$x_2 = (-a + b) / (a^2 - b^2)$ ... $a^2 - b^2$ is two square differences:

$x_2 = -(a - b) / ((a - b)(a + b))$ ... $(a - b)$ terms cancel each other:

$x_2 = -1/(a + b)$

39. A
To simplify, we need to remove the parenthesis and see if any terms cancel:

$(a + b)(x + y) + (a - b)(x - y) - (ax + by) = ax + ay + bx + by + ax - ay - bx + by - ax - by$

By writing similar terms together:

$= ax + ax - ax + bx - bx + ay - ay + by + by - by$ ... + terms cancel - terms:

$= ax + by$

40. C

We are asked to add polynomials A + B. By paying attention to the sign distribution; we write the polynomials and operate:

$A + B = (4x^5 - 2x^2 + 3x - 2) + (-3x^4 - 5x^2 - 4x + 5)$

$= 4x^5 - 2x^2 + 3x - 2 - 3x^4 - 5x^2 - 4x + 5$ ... Writing similar terms together:

$= 4x^5 - 3x^4 - 2x^2 - 5x^2 + 3x - 4x - 2 + 5$ ... Operating within similar terms:

$= 4x^5 - 3x^4 - 7x^2 - x + 3$

College Level

41. B

Total Volume = Volume of large cylinder - Volume of small cylinder

Volume of a cylinder = area of base • height = $\pi r^2 \cdot h$

Total Volume = $(\pi \cdot 12^2 \cdot 10) - (\pi \cdot 6^2 \cdot 5) = 1440\pi - 180\pi$

$= 1260\pi$ in^3

42. D

$\log_{1/2} x = 4$ ... We know that $\log_a a^b = b \cdot \log_a a = b \cdot 1 = b$
$\log_{1/2} x = \log_{1/2} (1/2)^4$ ... Now, we can remove $\log_{1/2}$ terms since both sides have this function applied:

$x = (1/2)^4$

$x = 1^4 / 2^4$

$x = 1/16$

43. A

If we know the coordinates of two points on a line, we can find the slope (m) with the below formula:

$m = (y_2 - y_1)/(x_2 - x_1)$ where (x_1, y_1) represent the coordinates of one point and (x_2, y_2) the other.

In this question:

$(-9, 6) : x_1 = -9, y_1 = 6$

$(18, -18) : x_2 = 18, y_2 = -18$

Inserting these values into the formula:

$m = (-18 - 6)/(18 - (-9)) = (-24)/(27)$ ... Simplifying by 3:

$m = -8/9$

44. C

We are given that,
$a_2 = 6$

$a_{n+1} = 1 - a_n$

Starting from the second term, we can reach the fourth term:

$n = 2 ... a_3 = 1 - a_2 = 1 - 6 = -5$

$n = 3 ... a_4 = 1 - a_3 = 1 - (-5) = 1 + 5 = 6$

45. A

If we know the coordinates of two points on a line, we can find the slope (m) with the below formula:
$m = (y_2 - y_1)/(x_2 - x_1)$ where (x_1, y_1) represent the coordinates of one point and (x_2, y_2) the other.

In this question:

$(-4, y_1) : x_1 = -4, y_1 =$ we will find

$(-8, 7) : x_2 = -8, y_2 = 7$

$m = -7/4$

Inserting these values into the formula:

$-7/4 = (7 - y_1)/(-8 - (-4))$

$-7/4 = (7 - y_1)/(-8 + 4)$

$7/(-4) = (7 - y_1)/(-4)$ ... Simplifying the denominators of both sides by -4:

$7 = 7 - y_1$

$0 = -y_1$

$y_1 = 0$

46. D
The area of a rectangle is found by multiplying the width to the length. If we call these sides with "a" and "b"; the area is = a•b.

We are given that a•b = 20 cm^2 ... Equation I

One side is increased by 1 and the other by 2 cm. So new side lengths are "a + 1" and "b + 2".

The new area is (a + 1)(b + 2) = 35 cm^2 ... Equation II

Using equations I and II, we can find a and b:

ab = 20

(a + 1)(b + 2) = 35 ... We need to distribute the terms in parenthesis:

ab + 2a + b + 2 = 35

We can insert ab = 20 to the above equation:

20 + 2a + b + 2 = 35

2a + b = 35 - 2 - 20

2a + b = 13 ... This is one equation with two unknowns. We need to use another information to have two equations with two unknowns which leads us to the solution. We know that ab = 20. So, we can use a = 20/b:

2(20/b) + b = 13

40/b + b = 13 ... We equate all denominators to "b" and eliminate it:

40 + b^2 = 13b

b2 - 13b + 40 = 0 ... We can use the roots by factoring. We try to separate the middle term -13b to find common factors with b2 and 40 separately:

b2 - 8b - 5b + 40 = 0 ... Here, we see that b is a common factor for b2 and -8b, and -5 is a common factor for -5b and 40:

b(b - 8) - 5(b - 8) = 0 Here, we have b times b - 8 and -5 times b - 8 summed up. This means that we have b - 5 times b - 8:

(b - 5)(b - 8) = 0

This is true when either or both of the expressions in the parenthesis are equal to zero:

b - 5 = 0 ... b = 5

b - 8 = 0 ... b = 8

So we have two values for b which means we have two values for a as well. In order to find a, we can use any equation we have. Let us use a = 20/b.

If b = 5, a = 20/b → a = 4

If b = 8, a = 20/b → a = 2.5

So, (a, b) pairs for the sides of the original rectangle are: (4, 5) and (2.5, 8). These are found in (b) and (c) answer choices.

47. B
$\log_{10} 10,000 = x$ ... We know that $\log_a a^b = b \cdot \log_a a = b \cdot 1 = b$

$\log_{10} 10,000 = \log_{10} 10^x$ Now, we can remove $\log_{1/2}$ terms since both sides have this function applied:

$10,000 = 10^x$

$10^4 = 10^x$ If bases are the same, powers are the same:

$4 = x$

$x = 4$

48. D
The distance between two points is found by $= [(x_2 - x_1)^2 + (y_2 - $

$y_1)^2]^{1/2}$

In this question:

$(18, 12) : x_1 = 18, y_1 = 12$

$(9, -6) : x_2 = 9, y_2 = -6$

Distance= $[(9 - 18)^2 + (-6 - 12)^2]^{1/2}$

$= [(-9)^2 + (-18)^2]^{1/2}$

$= (9^2 + 2^2 \cdot 9^2)^{1/2}$

$= (9^2(1 + 5))^{1/2}$ ... We can take 9 out of the square root:

$= 9 \cdot 6^{1/2}$

$= 9\sqrt{6}$

$= 9 \cdot 2.45$

$= 22.04$

The distance is approximately 22 units.

49. D
To understand this question better, let us draw a right triangle by writing the given data on it:

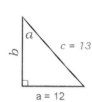

The side opposite angle a is named by a.
sin a = length of the opposite side / length of the hypotenuse = 12/13 is given.

cos a = length of the adjacent side / length of the hypotenuse = b/13

We use the Pythagorean Theorem to find the value of b:

(Hypotenuse)^2 = (Opposite Side)^2 + (Adjacent Side)^2

$c^2 = a^2 + b^2$

$13^2 = 12^2 + b^2$

$169 = 144 + b^2$

$b^2 = 169 - 144$

$b^2 = 25$

$b = 5$

So;
$\cos a = b/13 = 5/13$

50. D
$1/(4x - 2) = 5/6$ ... We can do cross multiplication:

$5(4x - 2) = 1 \cdot 6$ ... Now, we distribute 5 to the parenthesis:

$20x - 10 = 6$ ... We need x term alone on one side:

$20x = 6 + 10$

$20x = 16$ ... Dividing both sides by 20:

$x = 16/20$ ... Simplifying by 2 and having 10 in the denominator provides us finding the decimal equivalent of x:

$x = 8/10 = 0.8$

51. B
If we know the coordinates of two points on a line, we can find the slope (m) with the below formula:
$m = (y_2 - y_1)/(x_2 - x_1)$ where (x_1, y_1) represent the coordinates of one point and (x_2, y_2) the other.

In this question:

$(-4, -4) : x_1 = -4, y_1 = -4$

$(-1, 2) : x_2 = -1, y_2 = 2$

Inserting these values into the formula:

$m = (2 - (-4))/(-1 - (-4)) = (2 + 4)/(-1 + 4) = 6/3$ ... Simplifying by 3:

$m = 2$

52. A
The formula of the volume of cylinder is the base area multiplied by the height. As the formula:

Volume of a cylinder = $\pi r^2 h$. Where π is 3.142, r is radius of the cross sectional area, and h is the height.

We know that the diameter is 5 meters, so the radius is 5/2 = 2.5 meters.

The volume is: $V = 3.142 \cdot 2.5^2 \cdot 12 = 235.65$ m^3.

53. C
We are given that,

$a_2 = 3$

$a_{n+1} = -a_{n-1}$

Let us insert n = 2:

$a_3 = -a_4$ ... If we carry a_4 to left side:

$a_3 + a_4 = 0$ ... We were asked to find this. Without using a_2 = 3, which would not be useful in this question; we reached this result.

54. C
The large cube is made up of 8 smaller cubes with 5 cm sides. The volume of a cube is found by the third power of the length of one side.

Volume of the large cube = Volume of the small cube•8

$= (5^3) \cdot 8 = 125 \cdot 8$

$= 1000$ cm^3

There is another solution for this question. Find the side length of the large cube. There are two cubes rows with 5 cm length for each. So, one side of the large cube is 10 cm.

The volume of this large cube is equal to $10^3 = 1000$ cm^3

55. A
First write the two equations one under the other. Our aim is to multiply equations with appropriate factors to eliminate one unknown and find the other, and then find the eliminated one using the found value.

-$\sqrt{5}$/ x$\sqrt{5}$ - y = $\sqrt{5}$ ... If we multiply this equation by $\sqrt{5}$, y terms will cancel each other:

$x - y\sqrt{5} = 5$

$-x\sqrt{5}\sqrt{5} + y\sqrt{5} = -\sqrt{5}\sqrt{5}$ ... using $\sqrt{5}\sqrt{5} = 5$:

$x - y\sqrt{5} = 5$

$-5x + y\sqrt{5} = -5$

$x - y\sqrt{5} = 5$ ... Summing side-by-side:

$-5x + y\sqrt{5} + x - y\sqrt{5} = -5 + 5$ ... $+ y\sqrt{5}$ and $- y\sqrt{5}$, -5 and $+ 5$ cancel each other:

$-4x = 0$

$x = 0$

Now, using either of the equations gives us the value of y. Let us choose equation 1:

$x\sqrt{5} - y = \sqrt{5}$

$0\sqrt{5} - y = \sqrt{5}$

$-y = \sqrt{5}$

$y = -\sqrt{5}$

The solution to the system is $(0, -\sqrt{5})$

56. D

As shown in the figure, two parallel lines intersecting with a third line with angle of 75°.

$x = 75°$ (corresponding angles)

$x + y = 180°$ (supplementary angles) ... inserting the value of x here:

$y = 180° - 75°$
$y = 105°$

57. B

To understand this question better, let us draw a right triangle by writing the given data on it:

The side opposite to angle α is named by a.
The side opposite to angle β is named by b.
The hypotenuse which is the opposite side to
90° angle is named by c.

We are asked to find $(\sin α + \cos β)/(tgα + ctgβ)$.

As general formulas:

sinx = length of the opposite side / length of the hypotenuse

cosx = length of the adjacent side / length of the hypotenuse

tgx = length of the opposite side / length of the adjacent side

ctgx = length of the adjacent side / length of the opposite side

So, in this question;

$\sin α = a/c$, $\cos β = a/c$, $tgα = a/b$, $ctgβ = a/b$

Inserting all known values:

$(\sin α + \cos β)/(tgα + ctgβ) = (a/c + a/c)/(a/b + a/b) = (2a/c)/(2a/b) = (2a/c)(b/2a)$ Simplifying by 2a:

$= b/c$

58. D
Two parallel lines (m & side AB) intersected by side AC. This means that 50° and a angles are interior angles. So:
a = 50° (interior angles).

59. D
We have a circle given with diameter 8 cm and a square located within the circle. We are asked to find the area of the circle for which we only need to know the length of the radius that is the half of the diameter.
Area of circle = $πr^2$ ... r = 8/2 = 4 cm

Area of circle = $π•4^2$

= 16π cm² ... As we notice, the inner square has no role in this question.

60. C
We see that two legs of a right triangle form by Peter's movements and we are asked to find the length of the hypotenuse. We use the Pythagorean Theorem:

(Hypotenuse)² = (Perpendicular)² + (Base)²

$h^2 = a^2 + b^2$

Given: $3^2 + 4^2 = h^2$

$h^2 = 9 + 16$

$h = \sqrt{25}$

$h = 5$

Sentence Skills

1. D
"Who" is correct because the question uses an active construction. "To whom was first place given?" is passive construction.

2. D
"Which" is correct, because the files are objects and not people.

3. C
The simple present tense, "rises," is correct.

4. A
"Lie" does not require a direct object, while "lay" does. The old woman might lie on the couch, which has no direct object, or she might lay the book down, which has the direct object, "the book."

5. D
The simple present tense, "falls," is correct because it is repeated action.

6. A
The present progressive, "building models," is correct in this sentence; it is required to match the other present progressive verbs.

7. C
Past Perfect tense describes a completed action in the past, before another action in the past.

8. D
The preposition "to" is the correct preposition to use with "bring."

9. D
"Laid" is the past tense.

10. A
This is a past unreal conditional sentence. It requires an 'if' clause and a result clause, and either clause can appear first. The 'if' clause uses the past perfect, while the result clause uses the past participle.

11. C
"But replaces "though" and must be followed by the subject "they."

12. C
"Unlike" modifies and must be closest to "green tea," which is the subject of the sentence.

13. A
"Even though" has already replaced "but"; "shark teeth, the antecedent of "they," must then begin the main clause.

14. A
"Without" substitutes for "missing."

15. A
The order is: appetizer, and then main course. "Before..." is an adverbial phrase that must modify (be close to) "Antoine ate."

16. D
The "spotting" must happen "as" Katie skates.

17. B
"Eating" must modify "bears," which must initiate a main

clause.

18. B
The comparison opened by "more rarely" must close with a "than" phrase.

19. C
"Because" offers the reason for Jeremy's condition and does so grammatically.

20. A
"Nonetheless" replaces "but," and "wishing" must modify (be closest to) "Claire."

Conclusion

C ONGRATULATIONS! You have made it this far because you have applied yourself diligently to practicing for the exam and no doubt improved your potential score considerably! Getting into a good school is a huge step in a journey that might be challenging at times but will be many times more rewarding and fulfilling. That is why being prepared is so important.

Good Luck!

FREE Ebook Version

Download a FREE Ebook version

Suitable for tablets, iPad, iPhone, or any smart phone.

Go to
http://tinyurl.com/my73eyo

Register for Free Updates and More Practice Test Questions

Register your purchase at www.test-preparation.ca/register.html for fast and convenient access to updates, errata, free test tips and more practice test questions.

ACCUPLACER Test Strategy!

Learn to increase your score using time-tested secrets for answering multiple choice questions!

This practice book has everything you need to know about answering multiple choice questions on a standardized test!

You will learn 12 strategies for answering multiple choice questions and then practice each strategy with over 45 reading comprehension multiple choice questions, with extensive commentary from exam experts!

Maybe you have read this kind of thing before, and maybe feel you don't need it, and you are not sure if you are going to buy this Book.

Remember though, it only a few percentage points divide the PASS from the FAIL students.

Even if our multiple choice strategies increase your score by a few percentage points, isn't that worth it?

Go to https://www.createspace.com/4600491

Enter code LYFZGQB5 for 25% off!

Get Organized, Study Less and Get Higher Marks!

Here is what you will learn:

- How to Organize your Study Space

- Four different strategies for taking notes

- Reading strategies for textbooks, essays, novels and literature

- How to Concentrate - What is concentration and how do you do it!

- Using Flash Cards - Complete guide to using flash cards including the Leitner method.

and LOT more... Including time management, sleep, nutrition, motivation, brain food, procrastination, study schedules and more!

Go to https://www.createspace.com/4060298

Enter Code LYFZGQB5 for 25% off!

Endnotes

Reading Comprehension passages where noted below are used under the Creative Commons Attribution-ShareAlike 3.0 License

http://en.wikipedia.org/wiki/Wikipedia:Text_of_Creative_Commons_Attribution-ShareAlike_3.0_Unported_License

[1] Thunderstorm. In *Wikipedia*. Retrieved November 12, 2010 from en.wikipedia.org/wiki/Thunderstorm.
[2] Cloud. In *Wikipedia*. Retrieved November 12, 2010 from http://en.wikipedia.org/wiki/Clouds.
[3] Lightning. In *Wikipedia*. Retrieved November 12, 2010 from http://en.wikipedia.org/wiki/Lightning.
[4] Mythology. In *Wikipedia*. Retrieved November 12, 2010 from en.wikipedia.org/wiki/Mythology.
[5] U.S. Navy Seal. In *Wikipedia*. Retrieved November 12, 2010 from en.wikipedia.org/wiki/United_States_Navy_SEALs.

CPSIA information can be obtained at www.ICGtesting.com
Printed in the USA
LVOW10s1616230915

455410LV00016B/1372/P